CELTIC CYCLES

Guidance from the Soul on the Spiritual Journey

ANN LOOMIS

BALBOA.
PRESS

A DIVISION OF HAY HOUSE

Balboa Press books may be ordered through booksellers or by contacting:

Balboa Press
A Division of Hay House
1663 Liberty Drive
Bloomington, IN 47403
www.balboapress.com
1 (877) 407-4847

Because of the dynamic nature of the Internet, any web addresses or links contained in this book may have changed since publication and may no longer be valid. The views expressed in this work are solely those of the author and do not necessarily reflect the views of the publisher, and the publisher hereby disclaims any responsibility for them.

The author of this book does not dispense medical advice or prescribe the use of any technique as a form of treatment for physical, emotional, or medical problems without the advice of a physician, either directly or indirectly. The intent of the author is only to offer information of a general nature to help you in your quest for emotional and spiritual well-being. In the event you use any of the information in this book for yourself, which is your constitutional right, the author and the publisher assume no responsibility for your actions.

Any people depicted in stock imagery provided by Thinkstock are models, and such images are being used for illustrative purposes only.
Certain stock imagery © Thinkstock.

ISBN: 978-1-4525-9674-7 (sc)
ISBN: 978-1-4525-9675-4 (e)

Library of Congress Control Number: 2014907576

Printed in the United States of America.

Balboa Press rev. date: 5/12/2014

To the evolution of the Divine Feminine

CONTENTS

Preface.. xi

- Author's Remarks
- Acknowledgments

Introduction xv

Chapter 1: Bringing Forth What Is within You 1

Chapter 2: Sowing the Seeds...9

- Cycle: February 1 to March 21
- Celtic: Imbolc
- First Chakra
- Ritual: Nature Exercise, Dialogue with Turkey, "Beauty and the Beast"
- Altar
- Affirmations

Chapter 3: Tending the Garden 17

- Cycle: March 21 to May 1
- Celtic: Spring Equinox
- Second Chakra
- Ritual: Water Meditation, Dialogue with Dolphin, "Hansel and Gretel"
- Altar
- Affirmations

Chapter 4: Celebrating the Sun 25

- Cycle: May 1 to June 21
- Celtic: Beltane
- Third Chakra

- Ritual: Flower Meditation, Dialogue with Possum, "The Wizard Gandalf" and "Huckleberry Finn"
- Altar
- Affirmations

Chapter 5: Honoring the Heart..32
- Cycle: June 21 to August 1
- Celtic: Summer Solstice/Midsummer
- Fourth Chakra
- Ritual: Heart Meditation, Dialogue with Grouse, "Jack and the Beanstalk"
- Altar
- Affirmations

Chapter 6: Seeking the Truth..40
- Cycle: August 1 to September 21
- Celtic: Lughnasadh/Lammas
- Fifth Chakra
- Ritual: Meditation on the Past, Dialogue with Swan on the Present, "Aladdin and the Magic Lamp" on the Future
- Altar
- Affirmations

Chapter 7: Perceiving with Soul 47
- Cycle: September 21 to November 1
- Celtic: Autumn Equinox
- Sixth Chakra
- Ritual: Third Eye Meditation, Dialogue with Owl, Reframing "Jack and the Beanstalk"
- Altar
- Affirmations

Chapter 8: Expanding the Imagination 54
- Cycle: November 1 to December 21
- Celtic: Samhain
- Seventh Chakra
- Ritual: Star Meditation, Dialogue with Hawk, "The Cosmic Earth Child"
- Altar
- Affirmations

Chapter 9: Lighting the Path 62

- Cycle: December 21 to January 6
- Celtic: Winter Solstice/Yule
- Eighth Chakra
- Ritual: Light Meditation, Dialogue with Crow, "Rapunzel"
- Altar
- Affirmations

Chapter 10: Shining Forth 70

- Cycle: January 6 to February 1
- Celtic Spirituality
- Ninth Chakra
- Ritual: Rainbow Meditation, Dialogue with Porcupine, "The Pied Piper" and "Goldilocks and the Three Bears"
- Altar
- Affirmations

Chapter 11: Spiraling the Cycles 77

Chapter 12: Sharing Soul Blossoms 86

- The Inner Banks
- The Whole Tooth
- The Carousel Horses
- Hibiscus Meditation
- Animal Dialogue
- The Moon as Muse
- The Goddess Creation Story

References 99

PREFACE

Rooted in my psyche is a wheel on which the cycles of the months and seasons turn throughout the year. No one ever taught me this wheel; it has always been there, perhaps as genetic material since one of my sisters also reports having it. On this wheel, the winter months are at the top with the spring months on the left turning toward the summer months at the bottom and moving to the autumn months on the right.

When I learned about the Celtic cycles and seasonal celebrations, I came to the realization that the Wheel of the Year is a natural law with which we have fallen out of rhythm at the expense of our souls. The soul has an affinity for this natural law of cyclical seasons and can give us guidance if we learn how to be in conscious relationship with it.

Writing about the Celtic cycles has been very healing for me and a source of great joy. Along the way, I have had valuable help from members of my writers' groups as well as friends and family members. I'd like to acknowledge and thank each of them for his or her specific contributions:

- Jane Leonardelli: Jane has taken several of my writing classes, and over the years, we have become friends. One day over lunch, I told her of my idea to write a book on the Celtic seasonal cycles, and with her enthusiastic encouragement, the seed was planted.

- Colleen Rae: Not long after the lunch with Jane, the universe responded with a shamanistic creative writing class offered by another friend, Colleen Rae. Under Colleen's able guidance, the seed of creativity began to germinate, and I had the beginnings of a book.

- Ann Burrus: Ann was a participant in Colleen's class, and later on, we became part of a writers' group together. Ann never failed to give me an encouraging word as well as many practical and creative suggestions. In fact, it was her suggestion that I write the dialogue among the animals in chapter 12.

- Nancy Tusa: Also a member of one of my writers' groups, Nancy shares my interest in the writings of Carl Jung and Jungian analyst Marion Woodman. With Nancy's helpful guidance, I was better equipped to incorporate Jungian psychology into this book. As a skillful writer and editor, Nancy easily spotted places that needed revising.

- Jane Krupnick: A friend of Nancy's, Jane joined the group to write about her adventures on her sailboat and other travels. Her writing inspired me to include some of my own travel experiences, as the soul is expanded through taking trips whether on land or by sea. Jane's questions about the more esoteric parts of my book led me to greater clarity.

- Barbara Barr: With her sharp intellect, Barbara also posed insightful questions in the writers' group. Her love for the natural world and its creatures was a tremendous boon. When I was writing the animal dialogues, for example, a very helpful suggestion from Barbara was to research some of the animals' instinctual habits.

- Carolynn Carson: Also closely connected to the rhythms of the natural world, Carolynn immediately understood what I was writing about. Her love for Native American traditions, as well as her understanding of Jungian psychology, was a good fit with my writing. Carolynn is a prime example of someone who lives her life by a natural law.

- Jennie Ratcliffe: At times, Carolynn, Jennie, and I would meet at a local café to collaborate on our writing and share our mutual concern for the wider natural world. Somehow, the act of sharing ideas taps the depths of the unconscious. Jenny is a master at this, and she usually came up with insights I never would have considered.

- Laura Dunham: Laura and I have several things in common—our background as Presbyterians, our devotion to the Divine Feminine, and a love of writing. We formed a writers' group, during which Laura wrote one book and started another! Her initiative was an inspiration for bringing my book to closure. Plus, she appreciated my humor.

- Joseph Asterita: When Laura invited her friend Joseph to join our group, I recognized and appreciated his vivid imagination, which encouraged me to use mine. He always made a point to praise the parts of my writing that he found particularly insightful.

Joseph has a logical mind and alerted me to places where my writing could be more coherent.

- Karen Ziegler: Like Joseph, Karen also offered astute observations about my writing. Her sensitivity to the feminine gave me the green light to write about this aspect of the divine. During the time of our writers' group, Karen won first place in an essay contest sponsored by a resource center for women's spirituality.

- Carol Shumate: When Karen took a full-time job, I invited my friend Carol to join the group, knowing that the fluency with which she writes would be a help to us all. While Carol came to the group late in the process of my book, I nevertheless learned from her many ways to enhance and improve my prose.

- Ruth Hamilton: As the manuscript neared completion, I thought it would be a good idea to ask some other people to take a look at it. Ruth immediately came to mind. It was her idea that readers try nonverbal forms of creativity. As the founder of Carolina Health and Humor Association and Arts Can Heal, Ruth practices ways to heal the soul.

- Dan Grandstaff: Having worked with Dan on a previous writing project, I knew that he would offer some creative ideas. At his suggestion, I changed the titles of the chapters to better engage readers in the content. Dan suggested ways to develop the interactive exercises and encouraged the direction of chapter 11.

- Martha Phifer: Just when I thought the manuscript was complete, my friend Martha came in and saved the day. Her comments and questions about some of the content forced me to go back through and add, subtract, and sometimes multiply. Martha is one of the best editors I know, and her revisions have made a huge difference.

- Lori Loomis: Along with Martha, my daughter-in-law, Lori, asked just the right questions and made the appropriate revisions to bring the manuscript up to a higher level. It was helpful to have the impressions of someone from her generation. She especially liked the meditations and exercises and recommends that other young people try them.

- Corinna Loomis: Another member of the younger generation, niece Corinna Loomis contributed the beautiful art pieces found throughout this book. To view her work, visit her new Etsy shop: www.etsy.com/shop/BREATHandNECTAR. Along with her art, Corinna teaches yoga to balance body, soul, and spirit.

I also thank my husband, Bob, for his invaluable help and patience with my computer angst. To other family members and friends who have listened to my ideas and found them intriguing, please know that you have influenced me in many important ways. My appreciation is boundless.

INTRODUCTION

Are you confused by the myriad of spiritual paths beckoning to you? Do you feel let down and disillusioned when they don't deliver what you're looking for? Are you at a crossroads in your spiritual journey and wondering which way to turn? If so, then you are not alone: many seekers today feel dissatisfied with their spiritual path but don't want to give up searching.

The good news is that you don't have to give up searching. Perhaps you only need to approach your search in a different way so that you can find the path that is right for you. Finding the right path doesn't mean you have to abandon the one you are on. Instead, it may be a matter of changing direction to allow your soul to guide you on the spiritual journey.

I once opened a fortune cookie that read, "Before you can see the light, you have to deal with the darkness." No matter how hard we may try to avoid or get rid of the dark, it is there nonetheless, and we have to deal with it. It may be that the dark or unconscious realms of the soul are putting up roadblocks that obscure the light. One way to balance the light and dark aspects of the soul is to bring the natural world into the search. If we fail to include nature on the spiritual journey, the soul is likely to feel impoverished rather than empowered, and we may as well turn around. Having its own interplay of light and dark, nature with its rhythms can guide us along the way.

Creativity is another way to balance the light and the dark within the soul. Although I encourage writing in this book, feel free to experiment with other forms of creative expression. For instance, you could gather together a kit containing sketch pads, water colors, and other art supplies to work nonverbally with the rhythms of nature. Creativity in whatever form is key for loosening the grip on beliefs that might keep you from finding your true path. Above all, be sure to bring along your creative sense of humor. This book is meant to be taken sincerely but not so seriously that you don't enjoy it!

One way I have made the book more enjoyable is through the use of personal examples and anecdotes. Some writers avoid the word *I* for fear of sounding self-centered, but I believe that the personal leads us to a more authentic spiritual path. We are each created as one-of-a-kind human beings, and if we minimize our personal stories as irrelevant, we are in danger of choosing a path that belongs to someone else.

When you delve into your own story, you will likely find that your ancestral heritage contains powerful clues to your spiritual path. As an example, a strong Celtic thread weaves through my father's side of the family. My father's last name—and my maiden name—was Buie, a surname from the Isle of Jura off the west coast of Scotland. Buie is derived from the Gaelic *Buidhe*, and even today, you can still find the name Buidhe in areas of Scotland near the Isle of Jura.

Upon leaving the Isle of Jura, my father's ancestors settled in the area of what is now Scotland County, North Carolina, where I grew up. The Lumber River, or the "Lumbee" as the natives call it, meanders through the neighboring counties. Named as one of the top ten natural wonders of North Carolina, the Lumbee is a dark body of water surrounded by cypress trees. It is not unusual to spot a snake coiled on the banks or slithering through the river's strong current. In swampy areas, dragonflies hover over the surface of the water and frogs blend into the mossy logs. As a visitor once commented, "You can sense the nature spirits all around this river, even if you can't see them."

Celtic spirituality holds that the ancient Celts possessed the gift of "second sight," enabling them to perceive nature spirits. Although most of us of Celtic origin have lost second sight, we can learn how to use it on a higher level. With second sight, we are seeing through the lens of the feminine principle, which is connected to nature, the instincts, the body, and the shadow aspects of the soul.

My own understanding of the feminine principle has been greatly influenced by the work of Carl Gustav Jung, the renowned Swiss psychiatrist and psychologist (1875–1961). The son of a Protestant minister, Jung observed that the dominance of the masculine principle had led to an imbalance, not only in the realm of religion but in many other parts of the Western culture as well. This imbalance prompted Jung to dedicate much of his work to exploring the dynamics of the feminine so that balance might be restored. Like Jung, and probably many of you, I grew up in a tradition that subordinated the feminine to the dominant masculine paradigm. Reclaiming the feminine soul has become an important part of my spiritual path.

Drawing on the Celtic seasonal cycles and the writings of Carl Jung, this book invites you to explore the role of the soul on the spiritual journey. Chapter 1 develops the concept of the soul more fully and outlines how to use this book. Most of the other chapters are in workbook format, offering you the opportunity to interact with your own ideas and experiences. In doing so, your journey is more likely to sustain you throughout the many twists and turns along the way!

CHAPTER ONE

BRINGING FORTH WHAT IS WITHIN YOU

If you bring forth what is within you, what you bring forth will save you. If you do not bring forth what is within you, what you do not bring forth will destroy you.[1]
—The Gospel of Thomas

The above quotation from the Gospel of Thomas serves as a foundation for this book. It is about bringing forth what is within the soul into the light of consciousness. In this chapter, we focus on the first sentence of the quotation, keeping in mind that in this context, "save" means "to heal." Throughout the book, we explore ways to bring forth the power within the soul to heal both ourselves and the earth.

While most of the book is interactive and experiential, some key terms need to be clarified before we begin. Take *soul*, for instance; this is a word that has been bandied about so often that it is even used to describe a particular kind of music or food. In Greek, the word for soul translates as "psyche," and that is the way it is used in this book. It is the soul, or psyche, that gives meaning to our experiences in the outer world. If we listen to the guidance of the soul, it will reveal the spiritual lessons we are destined to pay attention to in our lives.

In Carl Jung's model, the soul (psyche) has two interconnected levels: the personal unconscious and the collective unconscious. The personal unconscious is subjective, made up of psychic material from our heritage, family of origin, and religious tradition. When we reflect on our life experiences in order to make sense of them, we are drawing on the personal unconscious.

---

[1] The Gospel of Thomas, *The Gnostic Bible*, 62.

The collective unconscious is more objective and cross-cultural in nature, a vast realm of instinctual and evolutionary trends. When we read mythological or ancient stories—perhaps about a flood that covered all the earth—we are drawing on the collective unconscious. Jung considered the collective unconscious to be the source of the archetypes.

The word *archetype* comes from *arche*, meaning ancient source (the collective unconscious), and *type*, meaning universal pattern. Archetypes are timeless forms or patterns that stream from the collective unconscious into the personal unconscious and find expression in images. While Jung did not claim to have discovered the archetypes, he understood their power to shape people's lives as well as the culture at large. He even wrote that when archetypal forces are activated, their power can be compared to that of an atomic bomb.[2]

The mushroom cloud that resulted from dropping the atomic bomb on Hiroshima, Japan, on August 6, 1945, is an example of an archetypal image. With its smoke polluting the air and its explosive chemicals penetrating the earth's body, the mushroom cloud can be viewed as an image of the lack of regard for the sacredness of the earth. Jung might say that the mushroom cloud represents man-made power gone awry, without thought of the destructive implications.

I was born three days before the dropping of the atomic bomb, and the image of the mushroom cloud has been with me all of my life. For example, whenever I exploded in anger as a child, my family would say, half jokingly, "Well, you can tell she was born with the bomb!" Perhaps I was destined to be "born with the bomb" to contribute in some way to the healing of Mother Earth. If this is true, the question I ask is: "What does Mother Earth want from me and from all of us in this age of species extinction, decimation of the ecosystems, and erratic weather patterns?"

In part, the answer may have to do with memory, the memory of the soul of the earth as well as the memory of our own souls. In a newspaper article titled "Moving toward Extinction," writer Timothy Keim compares species extinction with the memory loss that comes from Alzheimer's disease. They share a common root, Keim writes, in that there are "holes in the ecosystem of our gray matter and holes in the web of life that keeps us alive." Keim goes on to assert, "What we are losing is the memory of the miraculous mystery of Eden with which we have been bequeathed."[3]

---

[2]   *Dancing in the Flames*, 223.

[3]   "Moving Toward Extinction," *The Chapel Hill Herald*, 2.

In response to this article, Jung would likely say that this instinctual memory, which dwells deep within the collective unconscious, is also in danger of extinction. He believed that there is a hole in the soul, so to speak, and that it is within the soul where the healing has to begin. One way we can bring forth healing from the soul is to practice the Jungian art of active imagination.

In each chapter, there is a ritual section to practice active imagination in the form of writing dialogues with animals. The purpose of writing the dialogues is to bring consciousness to the instincts, for animals represent the instinctual realm of the soul. Many people tend to repress their instinctual side because it feels shameful or selfish. Take anger, for example. We may feel angry and then feel guilty for feeling the anger! However, there is usually a powerful message behind any feeling within us, and dialoguing with the animals can help us to recover that message.

Writing the dialogues offers a safe approach to dealing with issues that might otherwise feel too burdensome to handle. You can write your dialogues with the animals I have selected, or you can choose your own. If you would like a guide for choosing your animals, you can do as I did and consult the book *Medicine Cards: The Discovery of Power through the Ways of Animals* by Jamie Sams and David Carson. In this book, the power of an animal is expressed as "medicine." The section titled "The Nine Totem Animals" has instructions for using a card layout to lead you to the animals that might have a healing medicine for you.[4]

To write an active imagination dialogue, begin by greeting your animal with a friendly word, such as *hello*. Then ask your animal a question or write a statement that will evoke a response from the animal. If your dialogue seems phony or uptight or if you are feeling uncomfortable with it, try using humor and wordplay. The playful use of language can help to lighten you up so your soul can enlighten you. Once you have made a connection with your animal, it will offer a message. Be sure to thank your animal for the message, and then ask if it has anything else to say. Let the animal have the last word so it can provide the final insight.

It is also helpful to look up information about your animal's instinctual attributes. If Bear is one of your animals, you should know its hibernation habits. If Snake slides into your dialogue, find out how and why it sheds its skin. If Dragonfly hovers over the waters of your unconscious, consider the large compound eyes that make its eyesight exceptionally keen. An animal's instinctual gifts can reveal much about the essence of its medicine.

---

[4]   *Medicine Cards,* 18–19.

And don't be surprised if your animal comes to you in real life because writing about animals can attract them into your energy field. When I was writing about Groundhog Day, for example, I spied a groundhog perched in my garden as if to invite me to go underground with him. The appearance of the groundhog illustrates Jung's concept of *synchronicity*. Synchronicity can best be explained as a meaningful coincidence in the outer world that corresponds to an unconscious state of mind. When you experience a striking synchronicity in the outer world, such as meeting the animal in real life just as you are writing about it, this usually indicates a need to bring forth the message of the synchronicity into the light of consciousness.

Perhaps you have heard of power animals from the shamanic tradition. In tribal communities, the shaman journeyed into other dimensions with a power animal to bring back healing messages for the community. In keeping with the shamanic tradition, you can call your animals "power animals," or in keeping with the Native American tradition, you can call them "totem animals." I have chosen to call them "spirit animals" because the dialogues are intended to spiritualize (bring consciousness to) the instinctual realm of the soul.

The body is another aspect of the instinctual realm of the soul. Whenever we hear the word *body*, we usually think of only the physical body, but in a wider sense, *body* can refer to fields of energy that hold guidance from the soul. The emotional body, for example, can point you to an emotion that is trying to get your attention. When we ignore the emotional body, we may experience headaches or other bodily symptoms until we get the message. Related to these bodies, or energy fields, are the chakras, usually described as "wheels of light." The chakras are psychic power centers connected to the endocrine system of the physical body.

Many of you may be familiar with the seven main chakras, which have come into Western culture through yoga. The first chakra is located at the base of the spine; the second chakra is in the pelvic area; the third chakra is at the level of the solar plexus; the fourth chakra is at the level of the heart; the fifth chakra is in the throat area; the sixth chakra is between the eyebrows; and the seventh chakra is located at the top of the head. An evolving belief—and one I've applied to this book—is that there is an eighth chakra located several inches above the head, as well as a ninth chakra that forms an aura around the physical body.

It is a common practice to apply a color on the rainbow spectrum to each of the seven chakras: red for the first chakra, orange for the second, yellow for the third, green for the fourth, blue for the fifth, indigo for the sixth, and violet for the seventh. For the purposes of this book, I have applied white to the eighth chakra and the entire rainbow spectrum to the ninth chakra. This is not to suggest that the chakras are literally these colors; rather, each chakra corresponds to a frequency on the light spectrum. As you interact with this book, you will have an opportunity to experience the particular quality of each chakra color. So that they are in rhythm with the natural world, I have aligned each of the chakras with a cycle on the Celtic Wheel of the Year.

Chapters 2 through 10 provide the seasonal timeframes for the Celtic cycles; note that they pertain to the northern hemisphere and can be reversed in the southern hemisphere. For consistency, the equinoxes and solstices are celebrated on the twenty-first day of the month in which they fall, although in actuality, they will vary a day or two from year to year.

Here's how the wheel turns:

- Chapter 2—The first cycle begins on February 1 with the celebration of Imbolc and ends on March 21 with the spring equinox. In this chapter, you will have an opportunity to sow the soul seeds that you will work with throughout the following cycles.

- Chapter 3—The second cycle begins on March 21 with the spring equinox and ends on May 1 with Beltane. This chapter is about tending the garden of the soul seeds.

- Chapter 4—The third cycle begins on May 1 with Beltane and ends on June 21 with the summer solstice. In this chapter, the sun is honored as a source of power for the seeds.

- Chapter 5—The fourth cycle begins on June 21 with the summer solstice and ends on August 1 with Lughnasadh/Lammas. In this chapter, the seeds blossom in the heart.

- Chapter 6—The fifth cycle begins on August 1 with Lughnasadh/Lammas and ends on September 21 with the autumn equinox. In this chapter, the soul seeds find a voice.

- Chapter 7—The sixth cycle begins on September 21 with the autumn equinox and ends on November 1 with Samhain. Here, you begin to perceive through the eyes of the soul.

- Chapter 8—The seventh cycle begins on November 1 with Samhain and ends on December 21 with the winter solstice. This chapter attunes the soul to higher inspiration.

- Chapter 9—The eighth cycle begins on December 21 with the winter solstice and ends on January 6 with Epiphany. This chapter heralds the coming of a new soul consciousness.

- Chapter 10—The ninth cycle begins on January 6 with Epiphany and ends on February 1, where we began. In this chapter, you have an opportunity to synthesize the soul insights that have come to you throughout the journey around the Celtic Wheel of the Year.

Depending on where you live, you may not experience the distinct change of seasons that we have in North Carolina. To this, I say use your imagination and adapt. In other words, if it's snowing during the spring equinox cycle and you can't quite resonate with my description of azaleas and dogwoods, notice what is there before your eyes and give thanks for nature's beauty and bounty in whatever form. You can even create your own Wheel of the Year to correspond to the seasons in your location.

In each cycle, you will learn how to set up an altar of meaningful images. For example, on my first cycle altar, I have an image of a Black Madonna. Black Madonna is an archetypal image of the hidden light of the soul that dwells in the darkness of the unconscious. Also in each cycle, there are sample affirmations, or short statements, that influence the perceptions of the conscious mind. Affirmations are not meant to be mindlessly repeated in order to ward off negative influences but to serve as a reminder that the wisdom of the affirmation is already within you waiting to be brought forth into the light of consciousness. Although I have modeled several affirmations, be sure to add your own so that they come from your soul.

Since the soul thrives on storytelling, both personal and collective, I have included fairy tales for you to interact with and embody. Fairy tales are powerful archetypal stories that can bring forth what is within you. In "Snow White and the Seven Dwarfs," for example, the dwarfs can represent the seven chakras, whose wisdom is mined from the deep layers of the unconscious. The Wicked Queen in this story can represent a roadblock that obscures the purity of the soul (as depicted by Snow White). The queen's "mirror, mirror on the wall" can be viewed as a psychic tool that reflects messages back to you from the hidden or shadow aspects of the soul.

Interactions with the fairy tales can range from responding to the questions that follow the stories, writing about their symbolism in your journal, or dressing up as one of the characters. I suggest setting aside a specific part of the day to interact with your chosen fairy tale, preferably when you are alone or at least have some time to yourself. You might want to devote one day a week to your fairy tale in order to integrate its archetypal message.

If you would like a guide for choosing your fairy tales, you can do as I did and consult the book *Inner Child Cards: A Journey into Fairy Tales, Myth, & Nature* by Isha Lerner and Mark Lerner. Like the animal medicine book, it has a set of cards with suggested layouts that can lead you to the fairy tales that might have something to say to you. The plot summaries in this book are particularly helpful for bringing forth the symbolism within the fairy tales.[5]

As you go through each cycle, you will likely have profound and sometimes confusing experiences. This is a good sign and indicates that Eros is at work. Although Eros has come to be associated with "erotic," it actually means relatedness. As an archetype of interconnectedness, Eros plays an important role in initiating the individuation process. With Eros, opposing psychic energies—such as those of the Wicked Queen and Snow White—begin to come together and you reach a new attitude. Without Eros, there is no individuation.

Contrary to popular belief, the word *individuation* does not come from "individualism" but from "undivided." In the individuation process, the split-off parts of the soul are brought into harmony with the conscious mind. As the longings of the soul come into the light of consciousness, you are developing what Jung called the "true self." Like the knot that adorns Celtic art, the true self interweaves the dark and light forces of the soul, bringing forth what is within you for healing and wholeness.

When you come to chapter 11, you will have an opportunity to explore the second sentence of the quotation from the Gospel of Thomas: "If you do not bring forth what is within you, what you do not bring forth will destroy you." This chapter shows how to revisit the cycles on the Celtic Wheel of the Year, not as a circle this time but as a spiral. A spiral ascends and descends and curves and curls without being closed. By spiraling deeper into each cycle, you can relate more consciously to the destructive forces within the soul that may block your spiritual path.

Chapter 12 offers a creative outlet for the psychic forces in the form of writing. As you will discover, writing is an effective tool for tapping into the hidden facets of the soul. My hope is that the writing pieces in this chapter will be an inspiration for you to write your own. Above all, may you be guided by the light, and the dark, within your soul as you search for the spiritual path that is waiting for you and within you!

---

[5]   *Inner Child Cards*, 19–30.

Spirit Earth

CHAPTER TWO

SOWING THE SEEDS

Cycle: Beginning on February 1 and ending on March 21, the first cycle is a period of time when the earth is dormant and some animals are hibernating. Like the earth and the hibernating animals, the soul also seeks peace and quiet during this cycle to prepare itself for new growth. This chapter shows how to sow the seeds of the potential growth that lies ahead.

Celtic: The Celts ushered in this season with *Imbolc*, a word that variously means "in pregnancy," "in the belly," or "ewe's milk." Imbolc honored the lactating ewes, who would soon give their milk to feed the new lambs of the season. Brigit was a Celtic presence who watched over the lambs, and her feast day on February 1 had a close connection to Imbolc. As a milkmaid, midwife, blacksmith, and poet, Brigit was an inspiration to the Celtic people. Called "the shining one," she was often honored with candles. As you work with this cycle, you can call on Brigit as a midwife for sowing the seeds of the dormant light that shines within your soul. The modern tradition of Candlemas recalls the ever-burning flame of Saint Brigit.[1]

First Chakra: Mirroring the glowing candles of Candlemas, the first chakra is a cone of light that flows from the base of the spine down through the feet and legs to ground and support us as we walk on Mother Earth. Psychically connected to the adrenal glands, the first chakra gives us the life force energy we need to meet the physical challenges of being human. Called the root or base chakra, the first chakra is also connected to the organs of elimination. The first chakra helps us to release or eliminate that which no longer serves us so that we can get to the root of an issue that may be blocking our spiritual path.

---

[1] *The Magickal Year*, 74.

The resurgence of interest in indigenous people is essentially about reclaiming the lessons of the first chakra. While we can't very easily return to indigenous ways, our separation from the earth has left us feeling like orphans. The first chakra provides an opportunity to reflect on our indigenous roots and reconnect with the earth as our mother.

Like the first color in the rainbow spectrum, the first chakra color is red. Dark red is associated with the female because of her menstrual and birthing blood. This deep red also burns within the earth. Below the earth's surface and the blackness of the soil lies this redness, holy and secret, the mystery of the life force.[2]

During this cycle, consider ways to connect with red:

1. Drink from a red mug and imagine that you are watering the roots of Mother Earth.
2. On Valentine's Day, wear red in honor of the Mother's love.
3. Rather than get impatient at a red traffic light, see it as an opportunity to relax.

Since red has the lowest frequency of all the colors on the light spectrum, practice slowing down during this cycle. It is no coincidence that the season of Imbolc is called "stay-at-home time." It just feels right to settle down in front of red flames glowing in a fireplace or wood stove.

Groundhog Day is a cousin of Imbolc and offers an effective way to honor this cycle. Legend has it that on February 2, the groundhog pokes its head up through the ground to see if he can spot his shadow. If he sees it, this means six more weeks of winter, and he scurries back underground as if he is afraid of what his shadow will reveal. Like the groundhog, we can "go underground" (into the unconscious) and reflect on our shadow even if we too have a fear of what we will find.

In Jungian language, the shadow refers to psychic material that has been repressed in the personal unconscious because it is not accepted by our family or culture. If you find yourself judging someone else, you might ask what you need to learn from the shadow that this person has cast into your unconscious. Although shadow material is often perceived as dark and negative, you might be surprised to learn that it can also be positive. As Jung observed, the shadow is 90 percent gold if we will but take the time to dig for the nuggets.

---

2   *Dictionary of Symbols*, 793.

Watching the movie *Groundhog Day* can be an entertaining way to dig for the nuggets and shift repetitive shadow patterns so that we don't relive the same old lessons. In the movie, actor Bill Murray plays the part of an egotistical and insensitive weatherman who is bored by the ritual of going to Punxsutawney, Pennsylvania, every February 2 to report on the appearance of the groundhog. This particular year, he gets snowed in, setting into motion a trick played on him by his psyche: he is forced to relive the same day over and over until he learns his shadow lessons. When he finally learns to care about others, he gets the girl he has pursued throughout the movie (played by Andie MacDowell), offering an example of the gold within the shadow.

In our Western culture, many shadow issues are lodged in the lower physical body. The wounding is revealed in our language; for example, how often do we say, "I can't stand this," when we experience discomfort? Some people develop arthritis in the legs, knees, and hips—the parts of the body that enable us to stand on Mother Earth and connect our body and soul to the Mother. Without the perception of the soul, pain can indeed be hard to stand because it seems meaningless, but with the soul's wisdom, we can discern the messages behind our suffering.[3]

Along with the challenges of living in the physical body, the first chakra is also about survival on Mother Earth. Stories from childhood can reveal much about our attitude concerning these survival issues. For example, when I was seven years old, I almost drowned in the ocean. My family owned a beach cottage called The Seabuoy, and every summer, we would spend a month there. One day, when the ocean looked particularly calm, I sneaked out with the intention of going swimming. Little did I realize that beneath the ocean's apparent calm, there was a fierce undertow that would sweep me further and further away from the shore! Fortunately, my parents heard my pleas for help, but ever since that experience, I have approached the ocean with a healthy dose of trepidation.

Then, when I was nine, Hurricane Hazel tore through the East Coast, leaving destruction in her wake. After Hurricane Hazel, there was nothing left of The Seabuoy but rubble. This experience not only taught me a lesson about the impermanence of material acquisitions; it also taught me respect for Mother Earth's power.

---

[3]   *Dancing in the Flames*, 173–174.

We humans have a tendency to rebel against the power of the Mother and to rely on our personal will. While this tendency has given us a strong sense of autonomy, it has also led to the development of a false self that thinks it has it all together. When we are in the grip of the false self, we may hold contempt for those whom we perceive to be weak, or we might develop grandiose plans that disregard the integrity of Mother Earth. The disastrous oil spills that threaten to destroy our ecosystems can serve as a warning of this grandiosity.

Some people deal with the false self by "going straight for spirit." Going straight for spirit means that we bypass the soul, acting like we don't feel shame for what we have done to the Mother. We rationalize our shameful feelings in our minds and then lose the ability to feel them in our bodies. The more we try to think our way through shame, rather than yield to the sensation of shame in our bodies, the mind/body split gets wider and wider until finally our bodily instinctual side is repressed altogether and becomes shadow material. But at some point, this false self will start to break down. The call then is to get in touch with the shame that underlies the false self.

The figure of the shaman is coming back into our collective awareness in part to teach us how to get in touch with the shadow material of the false self. The shaman takes a journey into the psyche to reconnect with the true self, the totality of psychic wholeness. The self balances the dark and light sides of the soul, but in our Western culture, we tend to reject the dark, resulting in a repressed shadow that expresses itself in disorders of the physical body.

The first chakra is essentially about listening to the physical body and learning to rely on Mother Earth's wisdom. This isn't easy because most of us were taught to rely on ourselves and to strive for material success. Our culture neglects the first chakra experience, leaving us feeling scattered and fragmented. The doubt, fear, and anxiety that we all feel upon occasion can likely be traced back to our feeling of separation from the Mother. Rituals can help us to reconnect with Mother Earth and to feel more grateful and grounded.

The ritual for the first cycle begins with a meditative nature exercise to sow the seeds of the soul qualities that you would like to develop during the Celtic Wheel of the Year. It then moves into an active imagination dialogue with a spirit animal as a model for you to write your own. If you prefer to work with my spirit animal, there are questions at the end of the dialogue to guide you. When you come to the fairy tale, you might want to take out your journal to respond to the symbolism or a sketch pad to draw an image in the story that strikes you as important. As noted in the previous chapter, you can choose your own fairy tale if you prefer.

Ritual for the First Cycle

1) <u>Meditative Nature Exercise</u>: On a piece of paper, draw a large square to represent the ground. On another piece of paper, draw four seed-like shapes. In each of the shapes, write a soul quality that you would like to sow during this cycle. It could be learning to trust, asking for support on the spiritual journey, developing patience, being more creative, or finding new ways to honor your spiritual path. Now symbolically plant these seeds by cutting them out and pasting them in the four corners of the plot of ground that you drew on the first sheet of paper. If weather permits, you can go outside and plant the seeds in the actual ground. Whether the seeds are planted on the paper or in the ground, they will be germinating during this cycle.

2) <u>Active Imagination Dialogue with a Spirit Animal</u>: My spirit animal for this cycle is Turkey, whose medicine is "Give-Away." The message from my dialogue with Turkey is to transform materialism into "maternalism," that is, developing trust in the abundance of the Great Mother.

Me: Hello, Turkey. I've heard that you're called the "Give-Away" animal. Why is that?

Turkey: I'd like to hear from you first. Why do you think I'm called Give-Away?

Me: Perhaps your message is for me to stop being so grasping and greedy.

Turkey: Are you grasping and greedy?

Me: At heart, I'm generous, but I tend to have a scarcity mentality. I believe that there won't be enough left over for me.

Turkey: Have you always had what you wanted and needed?

Me: Yes, but maybe that's because I use common sense with my money. I have a lot of common sense, you know!

Turkey: Yes, I know, but have you ever not used common sense and everything came out fine?

Me: Well, lately, I've started to detach from the outcome of my financial decisions—you know, just go with the flow of my finances.

Turkey: How is that working out? Do you have just as much as always?

Me: Yes, I have all that I need.

Turkey: And have you noticed that the spirit of giving is growing within you?

Me: Maybe so. Just the other day, I stopped at a red light and gave some money to a homeless person. I also sponsored some friends for the Crop Walk.

Turkey: How did you feel about doing this?

Me: I felt more connected, as though I am part of a larger human family.

Turkey: Good. You're learning that money is meant to be recycled.

Me: Thank you, Turkey. You're teaching me to be grateful for my bounty and to share it with others. Do you have a final message for me?

Turkey: Remember that whatever you do for others, you do also for yourself. Think of money as electric energy, and recycle the current-cy!

Reflect now on the root of scarcity. Does it come from a feeling of lack of support? Are you trying to do everything on your own? Do you ask for support, or do you think it's weak to ask? In asking for support, perhaps trust will develop between you and someone else.

In the Christian calendar, Ash Wednesday almost always comes during this cycle, usually in February. As the beginning of the Lenten season, Ash Wednesday calls us to give up something. However, when you consider that Lent has the same root as "lengthen" (the days are lengthening this time of year), you might also want to add something to your life. In the spirit of Turkey, what can you add to your life to strengthen and lengthen your sense of abundance?

3) <u>Fairy Tale or Story</u>: My fairy tale for this cycle is "Beauty and the Beast." Beast represents the dark shadow and Beauty the gold embedded in the shadow. This story is basically about transforming the shadow into the light of consciousness.

Plot Summary: In "Beauty and the Beast," Beauty visits a castle, and there she sees a mirror. The mirror says, "Through time—in your heart—you will see truth." Soon, Beauty has a recurring dream in which she meets a handsome prince. Instead of a prince, however, she meets an ugly and malformed beast dying by a lake. As her tears flow in compassion for the beast, she sees the handsome prince from her dream reflected in the lake. When Beauty breaks the spell with unconditional love for the beast, he is transformed into the prince of her dream.[4]

If you choose to work with "Beauty and the Beast," try this exercise. Using a mirror, look into your eyes and ask these questions: Who is the beast within me? The perfectionist? The drama

---

4   *Inner Child Cards*, 74.

queen (or king)? The victim? Can I accept the beast within myself, loving it unconditionally and with compassion? Then, with the help of the mirror, ask: Who is Beauty within me? The peacemaker? The listener? The wise one? The shining one? How can I unmask the Beauty within? How can I embody Beauty so that her splendor is revealed?

Archetypal stories like "Beauty and the Beast" ask us to look at shadow material buried deep within our souls. Whether you work with "Beauty and the Beast" or another fairy tale, use the space below to come up with some ways to interact with it so that your soul can speak to you.

_____

_____

_____

_____

_____

In working with the first chakra, we can reclaim the shadow memories of our indigenous ancestors so that we feel more grounded on the earth. As a practice in grounding, lumber like an elephant with its feet solidly planted on the earth or walk barefoot to connect with the earth's electromagnetic field. Without grounding, we tend to "lose our center," "fly off the handle," or appear to be "not all here." We feel separated from the natural world and from our souls. Creating an altar and writing affirmations can help to remind us that the earth is our home.

Altar

My altar for the first cycle is an old coffee table in the downstairs area of my house, which is on eye level with the ground. After adorning my altar with a red cloth, I place a white candle in the center to represent Brigit and her healing qualities. Red candles in each corner remind me of the earth's red magnetic core. An image of Black Madonna depicts the earth's dark organic soil as well as shadow material in the personal unconscious. Ruby and garnet gemstones symbolize the red power glowing within the earth.

Affirmations (Fill in the blanks with your own affirmations.)

1) I am grounded on Mother Earth.
2) My body supports me.
3) I am a seed of the source.
4) I own my shadow material.
5) My first chakra is filled with spirit-permeated red light.
6) _____
7) _____
8) _____
9) _____
10) _____

CHAPTER THREE

TENDING THE GARDEN

Cycle: The second cycle begins on March 21 and ends on May 1, a time of rebirth for the earth. My yard is a testimony to this regenerative growth: purple irises bloom in the backyard, and red, pink, and white azaleas blossom in the front. Along with this debut of flowers, the buds on the dogwood trees begin to pop open, adding a splash of white to the colorful sight. Like the earth, the soul is also beginning to bloom and blossom during this cycle. As you relate to the new life within your soul, imagine that you are gently tending a garden.

Celtic: The Celts honored this season of new life by celebrating the vernal, or spring, equinox. *Vernal* stems from the Latin root *vernare* meaning "to bloom." Whereas the earth has been sleeping during Imbolc, at the vernal equinox, she begins to awaken. It is probably no coincidence that the month of April, which arrives on the heels of the vernal equinox, derives its name from *Aperio*, meaning "to open" as in "aperture."[1]

Second Chakra: The second chakra is located about an inch below the navel and is psychically connected to the female reproductive glands. It is sometimes called the sacral chakra because the sacrum bone joins the spine to the pelvis. Since "sacral" comes from the same root as "sacred," you might think of the second chakra as a sacred womb. In working with this cycle, your soul seeds are being prepared in the womb of the second chakra to birth something new.

Following the arc of the rainbow spectrum, we come now to orange, the color associated with the second chakra. The primary symbolism of orange is that of a point of balance between spirit and libido. This balance tends to be upset in one direction or the other so that orange may become a revelation of divine love or an emblem of lust. It is an extremely difficult task to maintain balance between the spirit and the libido. According to traditions going back to

---

[1] *The Magickal Year*, 90.

the worship of the Earth Mother, this balance was sought in ritual orgy. Over time, orange became the color of lust. Dionysus, the god of "wine, women, and song," was said to be dressed in orange.[2]

As you consciously envelop your energy in the second chakra, consider what else you associate with orange. A carrot? A pumpkin? A coral reef? An egg yolk? In the space below, play with other images as you experience the quality of orange.

_____

_____

_____

_____

_____

The moon is sometimes associated with the second chakra because of its association with water and the emotions. Since the moon reflects the light of the sun, it is also a good tool to work with when you reflect on your emotions. You can work with the powerful full moon that comes between the spring equinox and Easter to help bring clarity to confusing or uncomfortable emotions. If you are trying to control others, having trouble forgiving, or living in the grip of an addiction, ask the full moon to help you bring light to these struggles. Imagine that you are drawing the moon down through the top of your head. As it descends through your body, ask the moon to pause where the emotion is lodged. Then ask the moon to take the emotion to the womb of the second chakra in order to birth it into a higher state of consciousness.

The second chakra provides an opportunity to bring awareness to all of our emotions. In our culture, emotions have become shadow material because we tend to think of them as weak, but emotion can be thought of as energy in motion (e-motion). Walking in the rain or listening to raindrops coming down on your roof can connect you to the watery nature of your emotions. When emotions start flowing, water may come in the form of tears. If you have trouble feeling emotions, think of something that brings tears to your eyes. Since tears are nature's way of cleansing the soul, it is important to allow the wet, salty tears to wash through you.

When we emote, we are tending the garden of the "emotional body." The emotional body harbors our grief, traumas, dramas, betrayals, and disappointments. As we express our

---

[2] *Dictionary of Symbols*, 723.

emotions, energy moves out of the unconscious, through the physical body, and into the conscious mind. In doing so, emotions are less likely to become stuck in the body where they can manifest in pain and disease.

Along with emotions, the second chakra is associated with sexuality—another major shadow issue in our culture. When you are working with this chakra, don't be surprised if someone who attracts you sexually comes into your life. This attraction might not be convenient, but the true self will stir up the shadow in whatever way it can in order to bring about slippage of the false self. For example, you might fall in love with the "wrong" person, especially if that person has qualities that are undeveloped in you.

Even though the self will use anybody and anything to keep the process of wholeness moving along, sometimes our defenses are working so well that we may stay in the false self despite the call of the true self. We might even get so caught up in the unconscious grip of the self that we have an affair with the person to whom we are attracted. Our culture is full of stories of public figures who have disrupted their lives by acting out with a perceived soul mate. The better choice would be to ask the self what it is trying to say through the sexual attraction.

One reason that the second chakra remains a part of our Western cultural shadow is its relationship to the feminine. For most of recorded history, men have dominated women and the earth without an understanding of the connection between spirit and matter. Rape, teenage pregnancy, pornography, pedophilia, sexual harassment, and prostitution—as well as trashing the planet—are all a distortion of the second chakra.

We usually receive our first messages about the sexual nature of the second chakra during early adolescence, and we can probably all recount stories. Here's one of mine. When I was about eleven years old, Elvis Presley burst on the cultural scene, shaking his pelvis all over the stage of *The Ed Sullivan Show* during prime-time TV. My older sister and I were mesmerized by Elvis, and we enjoyed swaying and swinging to "Jailhouse Rock" and "All Shook Up."

Not understanding the emerging archetypal energy of Elvis, our parents asked the minister to encourage us to shift our allegiance to singer Pat Boone, whom they considered to be a more appropriate recipient of our adolescent lust. Having a lustful crush on the cute young minister, we readily complied and then proceeded to swoon and moon over Pat Boone's "April Love" and "Love Letters in the Sand." While this swooning did help connect us to our youthful emotions, the message about suggestive swaying was not lost on us. (Is it merely coincidental that the hula hoop also became popular around this time?)

Given that the 1950s was a restrictive decade in our culture, Elvis's archetypal energy may have begun a collective descent into the second chakra in order to bring soul into matter. So that soul doesn't become frozen in matter, it needs to swing and sway through us. It flows through our conscious form in creativity: writing, painting, singing, and dancing. And many women today are reclaiming the Divine Feminine, who stands for a new level of soul consciousness that can hold the tension between spirit and matter.[3]

Ritual greatly facilitates the soul work of consciously connecting spirit and matter. Through the repetition of ritual, the archetypal energies are evoked, and the psyche gets an idea of what needs to be brought forth into the light. The ritual for the second cycle begins with a meditation and then moves to an active imagination dialogue with a spirit animal, followed by a fairy tale.

Ritual for the Second Cycle

1) Water Meditation: The purpose of this meditation is to clear the emotional body. Choose a body of water that you feel most connected to, whether an ocean, a river, or a lake. If you choose the ocean, imagine the swelling of a wave. Let your emotions rise with the wave, and release them as the wave crashes and rolls onto the sand. If you prefer the image of a river, let your emotions flow with the current. Or you can simply allow your emotions to be still, like the surface of a lake. If it is not possible to be near natural water, fill a pitcher and slowly pour the water into a bowl to ritualize the living water within your soul.

2) Active Imagination Dialogue with a Spirit Animal: I chose Dolphin, a creature connected to water, as my spirit animal for the second cycle. Dolphin's medicine is "Manna," or sacred breath.

Me: Hello, Dolphin. I've heard that you're an expert on breathing. Can you teach me how to get in touch with my natural breathing rhythms?
Dolphin: Sure, but first I have a question. Do your ears ever ring?
Me: Yes, but why do you ask?

---

[3]   *Dancing in the Flames*, 44.

Dolphin: Ringing in the ears is called tinnitus, and it could mean that you're not listening to your soul. When tinnitus occurs, be still and go into the silence.

Me: Please tell me how I can do that when my mind is so full of external concerns.

Dolphin: Okay, take a deep breath, hold it for a few seconds, and then pop it out like a cork. Repeat this exercise five times.

Me: How will this help?

Dolphin: It will quiet down those pesky intrusive thoughts. When your mind is less cluttered, you can then focus on a mantra.

Me: What mantra would you recommend?

Dolphin: "So Ham" is a good one. Silently say "So" on the in-breath and then "Ham" on the out-breath. "So Ham" means "I Am That."

Me: How about "So What?" I don't get the point here.

Dolphin: Do you remember when you sang "Breathe on Me Breath of God" in church?

Me: Yes, I remember that song. Does it have a message for me now?

Dolphin: Think of "Breath of God" as manna—or sacred breath—moving through you.

Me: Thank you, Dolphin. You have inspired me with both manna and mantra. Do you have anything else to tell me?

Dolphin: As you learn to "swim" through the waters of the unconscious, you will attune your sonar to the sound of your soul.

"So Ham," or "I Am That," is a powerful mantra. "That" refers to the true self: with each inhalation and exhalation, you are receiving and honoring the self in the present moment. If you repeat this mantra for about twenty minutes, your emotional tensions will dissolve into a serene rhythm, like the pulsation of ocean waves.

A joyful and playful creature, Dolphin can cheer you up when you are feeling down. In the spirit of Dolphin, tap into the trickster energy on April Fools' Day and play a prank on a friend or family member. Notice how Dolphin's mouth resembles a smile. To create an inner smile, imagine a crescent moon extending from the left to the right pelvic bones. Be aware of your pelvis as you move through the world, whether it is enjoying intimacy with a committed partner or swaying to the beat of a favorite song.

3) Fairy Tale or Story: "Hansel and Gretel" is my fairy tale for the second cycle. Hansel can be thought of as the masculine spirit of greening vegetation and Gretel as the feminine soul of the awakening earth. Or Hansel can represent the sun and Gretel the moon, since day and night are balanced at the spring equinox.

Plot Summary: Hansel and Gretel are abandoned in a forest, symbolizing the unconscious, and are left to fend for themselves. They are guided by a white dove and a white duck: the dove leads them to a candy house, and the duck helps them cross a river to get there. When they arrive at the candy house, they believe they have found heaven since they have been suffering for so long without food. Hansel nibbles at the roof (spirit) while Gretel nibbles at the window (soul). After they satisfy their hunger, an old woman who lives in the candy house puts them in tiny beds. When they awaken, they find that they are prisoners of the old woman and the candy house.[4]

The old woman can symbolize the negative mother complex, a regressive psychic energy in the personal unconscious that stifles new growth by planting seeds of doubt about the worth of creativity. She would like to destroy and devour the new life that Hansel and Gretel represent, but the old woman self-destructs when she attempts to outwit Gretel. Instead, it is Gretel who tricks the old woman and pushes her headlong into the fires of a large oven, suggesting the transformative strength of the feminine soul on the spiritual journey.

Along with new life, Hansel and Gretel stand for a preliminary form of the "inner marriage," a Jungian term referring to the balance of the masculine (conscious) and feminine (unconscious) poles of the psyche. Together, they begin to weave a more holistic state of consciousness. As you work with this fairy tale, imagine the archetypal energies of Hansel and Gretel dancing through your energy field.

If you choose to work with another fairy tale, keep in mind that this cycle is primarily about the feminine power of giving birth. In the space below, jot down ideas from your fairy tale that can guide you toward giving birth to something new on your spiritual path.

_____

_____

_____

_____

_____

During the second cycle, pay attention to what is coming to life within the garden of your soul seeds. It could be that your frozen emotions are longing to thaw. If so, let your feelings bubble

---

[4] *Inner Child Cards*, 65–67.

up from the deep inner waters of the psyche. Whether salty tears of sorrow or spontaneous tears of joy come to you, this call arouses in you the spirit of creativity and imaginative play.

Altar

For the second cycle, I place an orange cloth on my downstairs altar. Since I live on a lake, the location of this altar gives me a clear view of the water and the wildlife around it. In the center of the altar are white and orange candles to represent inspiration and creativity. Seashells and a coral gemstone express the vibrancy of the ocean, and images of eggs symbolize the potential of new life. Anything that reminds you of the second chakra will be meaningful for this altar.

Affirmations

1) I allow the living water of my soul to flow through me.
2) I express negative feelings in a healthy way.
3) I pay attention to the rhythm of my breathing.
4) I attune to my emotional body.
5) My second chakra is filled with spirit-permeated orange light.
6) _____
7) _____
8) _____
9) _____
10) _____

Ocean Spirit

CHAPTER FOUR

CELEBRATING THE SUN

Cycle: Beginning on May 1 and ending on June 21, the third cycle mirrors solar power as the sun slowly begins to warm the earth. The emerging fire of the sun can serve as a meditative symbol as you ask the key question, "How am I using my power?" In this chapter, you can work with solar energy to empower your soul seeds.

Celtic: In the Celtic tradition, May 1 ushered in the season of Beltane. The root of the word *Beltane* may be derived from *belos*, meaning bright and shining like the sun, and *taine* or *tan*, meaning fire. Fire formed a central part of the Beltane festivities marking the end of the winter half of the year and the beginning of the summer half. In many tales with Celtic roots, the beginning of summer and the end of winter were depicted as a contest between two rivals competing for the May Queen.[1]

The May Queen, a central image of the Beltane season, was a girl dressed in white crowned with garlands of flowers and carried in procession around the village. This flowery maiden represented a youthful feminine energy that presided over fruitfulness and fertility. The May Queen's partner was sometimes called Cernunnos—Lord of the Animals—and at other times the Green Man or Jack-in-the-Green, who emerged from the wildness of the woods wearing a leafy costume and enclosed in a cage of branches.[2]

The maypole, another central image of Beltane, captured the Green Man's spirit and contained his seed. To enhance the maypole's magic, a group of female dancers holding on to the ribbons would circle round and round, interweaving the ribbons in a pattern. The physical energy of their dancing, the drumming rhythm of their feet, and their circling motion were ways of "raising the power"—like turning on a generator to invoke the force we call electricity.[3]

---

[1]   *The Magickal Year*, 112.
[2]   *The Magickal Year*, 113–115.
[3]   *The Magickal Year*, 117–119.

Robin Hood and Maid Marian are two figures that capture the spirit of Beltane. Their relationship in the wildness of the woods represents an early union of the masculine and feminine poles of the psyche. Robin Hood embodies masculine ego consciousness as it attempts to relate to Maid Marion, the embodiment of feminine instinctual nature.

Third Chakra: The third chakra—also called the solar plexus chakra—is often associated with masculine ego consciousness. The ego is sometimes thought of in negative terms, as in the terms *egotistical* and *egocentric*, but in Jungian thought, the ego is the center of consciousness. In the best sense of the word, the ego can be likened to the power of the sun because it gives us motivation and energy to maneuver the physical world and to follow through on our goals.

Located just above the navel in the area of the stomach, the third chakra is psychically connected to the pancreas. Given that *pan* means "all," and *creas* is related to "creative," this connection to the pancreas suggests that the third chakra is "all-creative." Think of it as a flowering of your creative abilities to forge a spiritual path that will be true and lasting. Listening to the "gut" of the solar plexus is a good way to tune into these abilities.

The creativity of the third chakra is cognitive in nature and relates to the "mental body." During this cycle, you might want to use your cognitive skills to analyze the information you have received from the first and second chakras. What have you learned about self-empowerment from these lower chakras? Be sure to use your sense of humor to avoid falling into judgment or victimization as you discern from the third chakra. Remember that the words *humor, humility, humus,* and *human* all come from the Latin *humanus*, meaning "of the earth," and that in the end, we are all human beings struggling to live harmoniously together on the planet.

As we move along the arc of the rainbow spectrum, we come now to yellow, the color associated with the third chakra. Yellow is the most expansive and intense of all the colors. As broad and as dazzling as molten metal, yellow overflows the limits within which one tries to confine it. Yellow tends so strongly to brightness that it is often the vehicle of strength and divine immortality. In Chinese symbolism, yellow emerges from black just as earth emerged from the primeval waters. Yellow was the imperial color in China because the emperor was thought to stand at the center of the universe, like the sun in the center of the heavens.[4]

---

[4] *Dictionary of Symbols*, 1137–1138.

What else do you associate with yellow? A sunflower? A daffodil? A lemon? A yellow traffic light? A coward? Choose an image that you associate with the power of yellow, and write down your associations in the space below.

_____

_____

_____

_____

_____

As you work with the masculine aspect of the third chakra, consider ways to relate to the feminine forces of the natural instinctual world. Washing your face in May-morning dew is an effective beauty treatment, and you can even make a wish as you wash! You can also offer some personal item to the Divine. It might be a piece of clothing that is part of your *persona*, a Jungian term referring to the face or mask we present to the world to adapt to the collective culture.

To honor other dimensions of the natural world, you might call on the fairy-folk, as Beltane is the season when fairies are more likely to appear to us human-folk. Since the fairies are lovers of music, song, and dance, you might find them dancing in a ring, on a moonlit hilltop, or under the trees. Be careful, though, because the fairies are tricksters and might whisk you away to Peter Pan's Never-Never Land, a timeless realm from which it is difficult to return. Fairies have always known what Albert Einstein later discovered: time is relative.[5]

Fairies and other beings that are multidimensional do not measure time in minutes, hours, and days, but we humans cannot fathom life without the units of time. Time governs our day here in the third dimension of the earth plane; without it, we would never get anything done. And how the ego loves to get things done and have something to show for how we have spent our time! If you feel caught up in the "busyness" of linear time, consider asking the fairies for help.

Staying overly busy is one ego issue related to the third chakra. Another is seeking recognition, but continually striving for success can become a power trip, and then we are at risk of becoming too competitive and willful. We may also spend too much time ruminating about the past or worrying about the future and thus have trouble staying in the present. What are some other ego issues with which you can identify? And what would be hard for you to give up?

---

[5]   *The Magical Year*, 139–141.

The positive side of ego development is that we have evolved into autonomous individuals with free will. However, the ego has also given us dualistic thinking, reinforcing the concept that nothing is related. Our indigenous ancestors understood that everything is interconnected: plants, animals, minerals, humans, and the elements of earth, air, fire, and water.

Although we can't very easily turn back the clock to this ancient way of perceiving the world, there are some ways we can reclaim this interconnectedness. One way is to use our attention and intention to connect the individual ego to the "divine ego." When the individual will and Cosmic Will are partners, we can co-create a more harmonious world around us. The ritual for the third cycle can help get us started.

Ritual for the Third Cycle

1) <u>Flower Meditation</u>: Think of a flower that represents the third chakra. Consider the yellow daylily, which opens up to the sun in the morning and closes at night. As the daylily opens to the light of the sun, focus on enhancing personal empowerment. As the daylily closes at night, focus on reducing power struggles with others. Or you might consider the daisy with its deep yellow center surrounded by white petals. The white petals can be a symbol of the spiritual solar plexus. There is also the magnolia blossom, which in the South begins to bloom in late May and early June. The magnolia can provide a fragrant floral meditation symbol. Whatever flower you choose, think of it as "Flora," a Roman goddess who represents nature's beauty and perfection. Flora calls on us to unfurl the power within, as symbolized by a flower.

2) <u>Active Imagination Dialogue with a Spirit Animal</u>: For the third cycle ritual, my spirit animal is Opossum, whose medicine is "Diversion."

Me: Hello, Mr. Possum. Tell me, are you ever tempted to use your claws and teeth?
Possum: Grrr … sure I am. They are there for a reason. Want to see them?
Me: No, thanks. I don't mean to offend you, Possum, but you're just not very pretty.
Possum: Ah, so you like for things to be pretty? What happens when a situation gets ugly, say, between you and another person?
Me: I usually use humor. Rather than show my claws, I bare my teeth with a joke and a smile, and sometimes my opponent will even laugh with me.
Possum: Do you ever use humor to put someone down?
Me: That's not really my intention. I prefer to use humor to lessen the tension.

Possum: Does humor always resolve the tense issue?

Me: At times, it does, but at other times, it makes the issue seem less serious than it is.

Possum: So you can't use humor all the time, but it's your first line of defense.

Me: Yes, humor comes naturally to me, but if it's not working, I just use some other form of diversion, like changing the subject.

Possum: Have you ever tried being direct? If not, what are you afraid of?

Me: I'm afraid I'll be perceived as "difficult" or "negative."

Possum: Is that worse than being perceived as a "coward" or "conflict avoider"?

Me: There's no way to avoid conflict, but there is a way to avoid offending people.

Possum: What is that way?

Me: To honor their position and ask them to honor mine.

Possum: What if they won't? I'll bet you would get very defensive.

Me: *What do you mean? I most certainly would not!*

Possum: Oh? You could have fooled me.

Me: Yeah, I guess I do tend to get defensive when I feel under attack.

Possum: If getting defensive doesn't work, what would you do next?

Me: Can you offer a suggestion? I'm about out of ideas.

Possum: Well, you could do as I do and play dead to the attacks—you know, just pretend they don't bother you. That would really spoil your opponent's fun, and then you could declare yourself the winner!

Me: Thank you, Possum, but I suspect that's not your final word.

Possum: Remember that a win-lose approach is allowing the ego to take the lead. Being honest with yourself and others is the road to authentic power.

Children who live with constant criticism and are not allowed to express their needs may develop a "possum mentality." They later have trouble relating to the instinct of aggression, and it is then in danger of falling into shadow material. However, like all other instincts buried in the shadow, gold is embedded there. To bring consciousness to the aggression instinct, consider times in your life when you "played dead" to attacks. Do you still retreat from conflict and disagreements? How can you express your opinion without fear of attack?

Opossums are marsupials and hold their babies in a pouch. In the spirit of Possum, reflect on the new life that is being held in the pouch of your solar plexus. Taking belly dancing lessons, doing yoga, and practicing tai chi or qigong are good ways to tap into this new life. These exercises can ease the tension in the stomach area as well as release the cords of behavior patterns that no longer serve you. They might even help ease digestive problems so that your gut can better communicate with you.

3) <u>Fairy Tale or Story</u>: For the third cycle ritual, I chose to work with two fictional characters, the Wizard Gandalf from J. R. R. Tolkien's *The Lord of the Rings* and Huckleberry Finn from Mark Twain's classic story.

Plot Summary: With his staff of wisdom, the Wizard Gandalf is an emissary of the divine consciousness "over-lighting" Middle Earth. He warns Frodo, who represents the child spirit, about the power contained within the One Ring. The One Ring can corrupt the wearer and eventually warp the wearer's personality so that it becomes a vehicle and tool of the dark lord Sauron. One of the main lessons Frodo learns is that true power resides within the ring of fellowship—one's circle of friends and companions on the path of life. Thus, the Wizard Gandalf is a spokesman for the higher meaning of group consciousness and community life.[6]

If you decide to work with the Wizard Gandalf, ask if your soul's needs are being met by your spiritual community or if you are simply trying to adapt to the collective.

_____

_____

_____

_____

_____

Huck Finn represents a free spirit who rebels against the norms of society. His life is one of trial and error and the desire to live with the flow of nature's wildness. As Huck goes fishing with his animal friends, he learns to connect with Mother Nature. If you decide to work with the figure of Huck, ask how he can help you address any fears you may have about being judged by the rules of society. Can you trust the flow of the river?

_____

_____

_____

_____

_____

---

[6] *Inner Child Cards*, 62–63.

With its focus on power, the third chakra is sometimes equated with the negative father complex, the restrictive rule-giving judge who belittles the changes you need to make in your life. But perhaps there is a positive male role model from your formative years who has helped to alleviate these negative effects. When I was in high school, for example, an energetic and fun-loving male minister encouraged me to take more responsibility in youth fellowship, teaching me the value of leadership, and a male coach put me on the first string of the basketball team, teaching me the joy of playing competitive sports. Reflect on your own experiences in the space below.

_____

_____

_____

_____

_____

Altar

At Beltane, I adorn my downstairs altar with a large cloth that has images of yellow lemons and a smaller cloth that has images of birds, which are chirping loudly this time of year. Yellow candles beckon me to tap into the power at the center of my consciousness. A citrine gemstone adds a sun-like sparkle to my altar.

Affirmations

1) I am worthy of respect.
2) I am confident in my ability to resolve conflicts.
3) I choose win-win outcomes with others.
4) I make decisions that are in my best interests.
5) My third chakra is filled with spirit-permeated yellow light.
6) _____
7) _____
8) _____
9) _____
10) _____

CHAPTER FIVE

HONORING THE HEART

Cycle: The fourth cycle spans from June 21 to August 1, a time of year that has always felt magical to me. Mimosa trees grace the landscape with their puffy pink blossoms, and crape myrtle trees dot the countryside with their variously colored clustered blooms. Fireflies light up the sky at dusk. The beauty of the season may have been why I chose June 22 as my wedding date. To add to the magic of the occasion, my attendants wore dresses of varying shades of rainbow hues. At the time, I didn't know that the rainbow represented the marriage of heaven and earth, but on some level, I must have sensed that it was a symbol of unity.

Celtic: This cycle honors the heart of the Celtic Wheel of the Year, ushered in by the summer solstice. Sometimes called Midsummer, the summer solstice marks the longest day of the year. For the Celts, Midsummer embraced the potential unity of masculine and feminine polarities: "The Solar God, who personified Father and King at the pinnacle of his power, embodied the traditionally masculine qualities of energy and authority. The Lunar Goddess, meanwhile, reached a similar stage in her eternally shifting and returning cycle: she was the Full Moon of Summer in all her glory, the fertile and fulsome Mother and Queen."[1]

It was also during this cycle that the Green Man exhibited his more mature side. While he cavorted with the May Queen at Beltane, at Midsummer he became the Oak King, the vegetation spirit at its strongest and most regal. In the Celtic tree calendar, the Oak King's special month was June. The old Celtic name for June as well as for oak was *Duir*, a word that comes from the Sanskrit "Dwr" and is related to the English "door." "Duir" is also the root of "druid." Although there is little written about the druidic rituals, it is generally accepted that they were performed in oak groves. Druidic lore suggests that the rituals focused on the heart, which was considered to be a portal or doorway into the higher dimensions.[2]

---

[1]   *The Magickal Year*, 142.

[2]   *The Magickal Year*, 149.

Fourth Chakra: The fourth chakra, usually called the heart chakra, is like a door or gateway between the lower and higher chakras. Located in the center of the chest, the heart chakra is such a powerful portal that it can stand alone without being connected to an endocrine gland. However, most sources agree that the heart chakra is psychically connected to the thymus gland in the upper chest. As the seat of the immune system, the thymus gland is sometimes referred to as "the high heart," serving to keep us emotionally and physically balanced.

To attune to the heart chakra, imagine that it has two rays, one that shines downward illuminating the lower chakras, and one that radiates upward into the higher chakras. In this way, the heart chakra becomes a sense organ for the higher intentions of the true self. It points upward to where it is going and downward to where it has been, acting as a vessel that can illuminate past lessons as well as future intentions. Reflect now on a key lesson you have learned from the lower chakras, and then bring the lesson up to the heart chakra. If the lesson involves a painful relationship, visualize a gateway in your heart through which forgiveness can pour in.

Notice that when you move the "h" at the beginning of "heart" to the end, you get "earth." Just as the earth is being warmed by the sun during this cycle, know that your heart chakra is also being filled with the warmth of love, joy, and compassion.

As the fourth color in the rainbow spectrum, green corresponds to the fourth chakra. It is a green that interplays with red, like roses that bloom amid green leaves. In the Middle Ages, physicians wore a green robe, perhaps because they used herbs to heal, and even today, some pharmacists wear green smocks to dispense their drugs. Green is also the color of environmentalists, who press their cases politically through Green parties. The qualities of green suggest that it symbolizes hidden powers of Mother Nature, from whom we sometimes feel alienated.[3]

To recapture the healing essence of green, go out in nature and notice all the shades of green this time of year. You can draw the green images on a sketch pad or jot down your associations in the space below.

_____

_____

_____

_____

_____

---

[3]   *Dictionary of Symbols*, 451–452.

It is a good practice to listen to the heart, for it is at this level that we first hear the voice of the true self. The self often contains a paradox, or what Jung called "holding the tension of the opposites." At some point in our lives, we all notice this pull of opposites. For example, when I was finishing up my master's degree in English, I needed to choose a topic for my thesis. Since I enjoyed studying Shakespeare's plays, I decided to compare the farcical skit "Pyramus and Thisbe" within *A Midsummer Night's Dream* to the tragic play *Romeo and Juliet* in order to show how Shakespeare's opposing treatments of similar plots could result in either a comedy or a tragedy. In writing this thesis, I realized that life is often a dance of the comic and the tragic and it is in following the heart that we can learn the steps.

If you are listening to the heart, you will likely follow the needs of your soul rather than your ego needs. If you are alienated from your soul needs, the heart will usually let you know in the form of palpitations or a tight chest. Women, in particular, play the traditional role of downplaying their needs and serving others at the expense of their own happiness. Sometimes it may even take an illness or accident to force women to pay attention to the need for self-nurture.

If your heart tells you to nurture yourself, take time out to have a massage, a Reiki session, or some other form of bodywork to help release old, worn-out patterns that no longer serve you. These healing modalities can activate the "etheric body," a field of energy related to the life force. The etheric body stabilizes the emotional and mental bodies and holds memories of earlier times of our life on earth. When the etheric body is tapped in the heart chakra, it can bring back memories of what gave our heart joy as a child.

When I was a young child, my favorite toy was a red and gold Ferris wheel. It had a key on the side to make the Ferris wheel turn around and bucket seats for small doll figures. The movement of the Ferris wheel can resemble that of a healthy heart chakra, which revolves in a circular, clockwise fashion when filled with the joy of child-like play.

Like the Ferris wheel, the merry-go-round can also be a symbol of the heart chakra: the base goes around in a circular motion as if to bring all parts of the psyche to the center, while the up-and-down movement of the carousel horses mirrors the journey between the lower and higher chakras. Picture yourself now on a carousel horse. As you ride down on the horse, remember a favorite toy or activity from childhood. As you move up, bring the memory into the heart chakra and allow it to quicken with life-giving etheric energy.

The etheric body of the heart chakra often moves through the arms into the hands. In today's world, we keep our hands so active on the computer and with other busy work that we don't even notice the life force there. As you meditate on the heart chakra, notice your hands. How would you describe the energy there?

The heart chakra can sometimes be hard to access because it is blocked by painful memories. As you work with the heart chakra, resist the temptation to get stuck in rationalizations that explain away your pain. Feel the pain there, and soothe it as you would a vulnerable child. The ritual for the fourth cycle can help unlock the door to painful places in the heart that may be shut down.

Ritual for the Fourth Cycle

1) <u>Heart Meditation</u>: Imagine the heart chakra as having two intersecting triangles. The descending triangle represents energy flowing into the lower chakras, and the ascending triangle represents energy moving into the higher chakras. Now visualize a rose-pink color in the lower triangle and a light green in the upper triangle. Allow the two colors to mingle, creating sparkles of pink and green translucent light. Imagine this light forming a rosebush that radiates beauty into the world.

If you scramble the letters in "rose," you get "Eros," a word meaning relatedness. As an archetype that signifies a greening of the soul, Eros initiates a higher relationship between the masculine and feminine poles of the psyche, paving the way toward balance and wholeness.

2) <u>Active Imagination Dialogue with a Spirit Animal</u>: My spirit animal for the fourth cycle is Grouse, whose medicine is "Sacred Spiral." Just as Grouse moves through its world in an ever-widening circle, this dialogue is a spiral dance to reveal wisdom in the inner world of the heart.

Me: Hello, Grouse. I'd like to "grouse" a little if you don't mind—you know, complain.
Grouse: Sure. What's your complaint?
Me: I love to dance, but I don't go dancing very often. It's as if dancing isn't important.
Grouse: It must not be important if you don't allow time for it.
Me: Maybe that's what I'm grousing about, time for it. I can't do everything, you know!
Grouse: Yes, I know. But dancing is part of who I am, so I can't relate to not finding time for it. Want to grouse about something else?

Me: Like lack of time, for instance?

Grouse: Which kind of time—*chronos* or *kairos*?

Me: What's the difference? Clue me in here.

Grouse: Chronos is chronological time, calendar time—you could even call it cuckoo-clock time because it will eventually drive you cuckoo. Kairos is flow time, ocean-wave time, Margaritaville time. Tell me, when you dance, are you in chronos or kairos time?

Me: When I dance, I lose track of all time. Time isn't relevant when I dance.

Grouse: You have just described kairos time. Maybe your resistance to finding time to dance relates to your resistance to kairos time. What's behind that?

Me: I think chronos time gives me a sense of being in control.

Grouse: And then time starts to control you. That's what you're really grousing about.

Me: So you're saying that if I set aside time to go dancing, then I'll start living more in kairos time. I'll go put dancing on my calendar right away!

Grouse: Wait a minute! What about the inner dance?

Me: The inner dance? I think I need a lesson on this one.

Grouse: Okay, start by visualizing particles of light dancing in your solar plexus. Play with the light there for a while and then bring it into your heart where it becomes a swirling wave of light, like the Milky Way. Got that so far?

Me: Well, I heard what you said, but I don't know if I've got it right.

Grouse: Don't worry about "right." Simply release control and play with the light.

Me: Thank you, Grouse—my heart feels more open and receptive already. But before you go, do you have a final message for me?

Grouse: When you dance, allow your heart to be filled with both particle and wave, the very essence of light. There you will find "in-lightenment."

In the spirit of Grouse, dance outside in nature. As you follow the spiral of the Grouse dance, you begin to get back in touch with the earth's cycles; then you will notice the etheric energy, both outer and inner, that puts you in harmony with body, soul, and spirit. In this way, you can learn to flow in the moment of kairos time.

3) <u>Fairy Tale or Story</u>: My fairy tale for this cycle is "Jack and the Beanstalk." As Jack climbs up and down the beanstalk, he mirrors the path of the heart chakra.

Plot Summary: In the story, Jack is caring for his poor mother. Jack's mother asks him to sell their cow for food and provisions, but Jack buys some magic beans instead. His mother thinks the beans are worthless and tosses them into the garden. While she is weeping over their misfortune, Jack sees that a mighty beanstalk has grown up overnight, rising beyond the clouds. Jack climbs the beanstalk several times, visiting a castle in the sky inhabited by a giant. On his last trip, Jack seizes a hen that lays golden eggs and a magical harp that plays itself. As the giant chases him down the beanstalk, Jack chops it in half, causing the giant to fall to earth and die.[4]

The issue of surrender is strong in this story. Jack surrenders the cow in order to purchase the magic beans, signifying that Jack can no longer remain attached to the scarcity views of his mother. He trusts that a new, more abundant life will bloom from the sprouting beans. When Jack vanquishes the giant, he surrenders the internal stagnation that the giant represents and faces the fears looming large in his unconscious mind.

If you decide to interact with this story, remember that even a little enlightened imagination can help vanquish the inner giant that keeps you from your heart's desire. Imagine your spine as a "spiritual beanstalk" carrying divine impulses. This spiritual beanstalk has green shoots that symbolize something tender and fragile growing in your inner garden. Jack's magic beans can represent the seeds that you planted in the first cycle. The seeds are now blossoming into a triumphant plant, like a beanstalk, bursting forth above the ground and reaching toward the sky.

Another story that works well in this cycle is "Peter Pan." Imagine your soul as "Tinker Bell," Peter Pan's fairy friend. In the story, Tinker Bell lets Peter Pan know when his desire for freedom is ungrounded, and she also becomes agitated when Wendy tries to domesticate him. The soul is like that—it is forever striving for balance between freedom and conformity. As an image of the soul, Tinker Bell resembles a hummingbird with small wings that vibrate faster and faster when looking for nectar in the summer flowers. Allow Tinker Bell to bring the nectar of love, joy, and compassion into the etheric field of your heart center.

Altar

For the fourth cycle, my altar is on the main level of my house. I adorn my dining room table with a green cloth to represent the life force within all of nature. The expanse of the table reminds me to widen my heart. Daisies in green vases surrounded by green and pink candles

---

4   *Inner Child Cards*, 89–91.

provide a soulful centerpiece. On my altar, there is a round mosaic tile with an image of a heart in the middle of two intersecting triangles, like the Star of David. A whimsical figure, like Puck from *A Midsummer Night's Dream*, entices me to look for the magic in the summer solstice season. A rose quartz and a bright-green emerald add beauty and sparkle to my altar.

Affirmations

1) I honor my heart's desire.
2) I attune my heart to the needs of my soul.
3) Love opens my heart.
4) My intentions are pure in heart.
5) My fourth chakra is filled with spirit-permeated green light.
6) _____
7) _____
8) _____
9) _____
10) _____

Summer Solstice

CHAPTER SIX

SEEKING THE TRUTH

Cycle: Beginning on August 1 and ending on September 21, the fifth cycle moves into the waning part of the year. Although the sun is still intense, summer is coming to an end. You can take advantage of the dog days of August by resting from labor, but after Labor Day on the first Monday in September, it is back to work or to school. As a teacher, writer, and lifelong lover of education, I consider this cycle to be a time for new learning opportunities. In this chapter, you will learn new ways to seek and speak your truth.

Celtic: In the Celtic tradition, the celebration of Lughnasadh began on August 1. Lughnasadh is named for the god Lugh, a name associated with "oath." Among his many other gifts, Lugh was an accomplished warrior, and the Celts enjoyed playing competitive games in Lugh's honor. During Lughnasadh, consider what your "inner warrior" might be calling you to do at this stage of your life. It could be fighting for the environment or speaking up for some other cause that is important to you, as well as answering the call to seek a new spiritual path. In the spirit of Lughnasadh, make an oath with your soul to help you follow through on this calling.

Lammas, meaning "loaf-mass," was another Celtic celebration that came during early August. Lammas marked the first harvest, when many of the crops were plentiful. Having been born on August 3, I feel a special connection to the Lammas season. When my first grandchild was born, I honored this connection by removing the "L" from the beginning of "Lammas" and the "S" from the end to come up with "Amma" for my grandmother name. Amma was easy for a small child to say, and it identified a different way of being at this stage of my life—a harvesting of the role I had played earlier in my life as "Mama."

Consider the soul seeds you planted in the first chakra and what now might be ready for harvest. Perhaps it is a creative project, a change in a role you have played, or a turn in the bend of your spiritual path. You might even want to give yourself a new name to represent this new period in your life. Explore some ideas in the space below.

_____

_____

_____

_____

_____

Fifth Chakra: The fifth chakra, also called the throat chakra, extends from the thyroid gland in the hollow of the throat into the area of the ears. The thyroid gland is shaped like a butterfly, a well-known symbol of transformation. As the psychic seat of the thyroid gland, the fifth chakra is about transforming communication: learning how to talk things out without backing off from your truth, monitoring expression so that you can be heard, and knowing when to speak and when to listen. If you are feeling tension in the neck and shoulders, consider how you are sending and receiving communication. Taking singing lessons or public-speaking classes or simply humming throughout the day are good ways to activate the fifth chakra.

Many of us may feel stuck in the area of the fifth chakra because we don't know how to express our truth; indeed, we may not even know what our truth is! And when we get an inkling of our truth and attempt to give it expression, we may discover that others ridicule it or don't take it seriously. Some of us may even give up when we get to the fifth chakra. We might find ourselves thinking: *What's the use? The prevailing culture is in charge, and I have even sold out to it myself!* If you are having these thoughts, know that you are in the midst of a perfectly normal inner conflict. Since that is the truth as you perceive it now, allow it to have its say. The fifth chakra is about expressing your truth, not suppressing it, and in time, your voice will open up to its wisdom.

Following along the upper spectrum of the rainbow, the color for the fifth chakra is sky blue. It is a quality of blue that seldom occurs in the natural world except as a translucency—an accumulation of emptiness and purity as in the void of the heavens, the depths of the sea, or the qualities of crystals and diamonds. Blue and white, which are the colors of the Virgin Mary, denote a flight of the liberated soul toward the Divine, as is celebrated in the Feast of the Assumption of the Virgin Mary on August 15.[1]

---

[1] *Dictionary of Symbols*, 102–104.

As you connect to the spaciousness of the sky, consider what else you associate with blue. A blue mood? The Blue Ridge Parkway? Baby-blue eyes? Blue velvet? The bluebird of happiness? Carolina blue? How many songs can you name with "blue" in the title? Now choose a blue association and write your reflections in the space below.

_____

_____

_____

_____

_____

At the level of the fifth chakra, we may feel called to form a new relationship with the soul. If we do not pay attention to the yearning for this relationship, we are likely to "project" soul. To project is to place our psychic hooks onto people or objects, seeing in them what we cannot see, or do not want to see, in ourselves. Soul can be projected onto our religious institution, alma mater, house, car, and even our boat! Any of our relationships or material possessions can be hooks for soul projections.

The fifth chakra is about identifying and naming projections: we love the "god" in the other person; we blame the other person for our own darkness; we think the other person is the bringer of the light. The withdrawal of these projections transforms the other person into a real human being with needs other than our own. It is the acknowledgment of the otherness of the person that creates an energy field of love. When that field of love is established, a freedom enters the relationship, and gradually, it can be recognized as the freedom to love another without false expectations or dependency needs.[2]

When the soul first begins to call, the old authoritative, judgmental "father" may still be hovering somewhere in the background. But one day, we might meet someone who encourages us to find the authentic voice that comes from deep within the soul. If we do not listen to our authentic voice, problems in the throat, such as laryngitis or thyroid disease, may indicate that the voice has turned to stone. As Pythagoras wrote, "A stone is frozen music." This music longs to resonate through us, but it cannot express itself if we have lost touch with our own sound.[3]

---

[2]   *The Maiden King*, 218–219.
[3]   *Dancing in the Flames*, 156–158.

Recovering our sound requires the building up of the "subtle body" as a container for the light of the growing new consciousness that is being released through deep inner work. To experience the subtle body, imagine butterfly wings moving through you and within you. Be aware of your judgmental thoughts and entrenched attitudes when working with the subtle body. If you go back to old ways of thinking and relating that take the voice away, the subtle body cannot survive.

The ritual for the fifth cycle strengthens the subtle body by offering an opportunity to look back over the past, to assess the present, and to envision the future. It helps to harvest the fruits of the inner work you have done so far and to come closer to finding your truth. The meditation deals with the past, the active imagination dialogue with the present, and the fairy tale with the future.

Ritual for the Fifth Cycle

1) <u>Meditation</u>: Meditate on a past situation that has now been resolved. It might be an insight that has taught you a valuable lesson, or it may be that you have found a solution to an ongoing challenge. Perhaps you have found a way to deepen the spiritual path you have been traveling so far, or maybe you have found a new, more rewarding one. Think of something in your past that you want to honor now as a lesson that has brought you closer to the truth you are seeking.

In this meditation, visualize the fifth chakra as a blue lotus flower located in the hollow of the throat. Imagine that the lotus has an essence that can integrate body, soul, and spirit. To receive the remedy of this healing essence, breathe deeply into the lotus. Now take a walk in nature to open to the plant world that surrounds and protects the planet. As you walk, notice the variety of flowers, trees, and plants blooming during this cycle. Allow their healing energy to permeate the subtle body.

2) <u>Active Imagination Dialogue with a Spirit Animal</u>: Consider a present conflict or challenge that may be an impediment to finding your truth, and ask for help from your spirit animal. My spirit animal is Swan, whose medicine is "Grace." Just as conflicts have two sides, so does Swan: when young, it takes the form of an awkward ugly duckling, and as it matures, it becomes a graceful swan.

Me: Hello, Swan. I seem to be seeing you everywhere these days. What's up?

Swan: My feathers, for one thing. They get ruffled when I'm threatened.

Me: What's threatening you?

Swan: Do you remember the painting of me that you admired in an art museum in Amsterdam a few years ago?

Me: I sure do. You were in the center with your wings lifted upward trying to protect your egg from an aggressive dog.

Swan: Yes, I'm very protective of my egg. But what attracted you to that painting?

Me: Part of it was your outstretched wings, and part was the golden egg.

Swan: What does the egg represent to you?

Me: An egg represents potential. Something precious is contained inside the shell.

Swan: What about the dog? What does he represent?

Me: Maybe he represents something vicious that threatens the precious potential.

Swan: What is the potential that the dog is threatening?

Me: I'm not sure, but I do know that it's vulnerable to growling things, like dogs!

Swan: Okay, let's go back to the beginning of this conversation. You mentioned that you're seeing me everywhere these days. Other than the painting, where else?

Me: At another museum, you were featured as a silver swan that ducked its head into a bowl of water. Later, I saw you featured as a black swan on a pub sign.

Swan: Anywhere else?

Me: Not long after I got home, my husband and I visited friends at their lake house in Virginia. There were two white swans on the lake that let me feed them—that is, until my friends' dog jumped into the water and ruffled their feathers!

Swan: Could it be that your feathers are getting ruffled over something these days? And what makes you feel like ducking your head?

Me: I guess my dark side does tend to come out when my creativity is undermined.

Swan: Well, maybe you need to do some undermining of your own—you know, go under the dark waters of the unconscious to mine the gold of your creativity. Your dark side is simply a part of yourself that hasn't yet been brought into the light. It's "in the dark," so to speak.

Me: I wonder what hasn't yet reached consciousness.

Swan: Let's take a look at my two sides: the black ugly duckling and the white graceful swan. Which one feels more vulnerable?

Me: Definitely the dark duckling. It isn't as valued as the light swan.

Swan: Yes, it's the light side that people like best. But the dark duckling eventually turns into a beautiful swan, just as the night transforms into the day and the moon grows into glorious fullness.

Me: It sounds to me that I need to cultivate my dark side if I'm to reach my creative potential. Thank you, Swan. Is there anything else you'd like to say?

Swan: And it sounds to me that you are hatching the wisdom of your soul.

In the spirit of Swan, think of the conflict as a dueling sport of dualistic opposites: dark/light, inner/outer, masculine/feminine, or even good/evil. Such archetypal opposites are two sides of the same coin, and it is wise not to split them apart. Engage "both/and" thinking as you imagine a third thing being born from the dualistic pairs. Think of Swan's long, graceful neck as an empowered throat chakra that gives voice to the resolution of your present problem or conflict.

3) <u>Fairy Tale or Story</u>: Now choose a fairy tale or story that represents something in the future, a glimpse around the corner so to speak. My story for this ritual is "Aladdin and the Magic Lamp."

Plot Summary: In the story, Aladdin is sent by a sorcerer into an underground garden to obtain an old lamp, and the sorcerer gives him a ring to help him on his journey. When Aladdin finds the lamp, he discovers that he is unable to leave the garden. He accidentally rubs the ring and a genie appears, granting him several wishes. Aladdin then makes a wish to leave the garden, and he instantly returns to his mother's house. When his mother tries to sell the lamp to buy food, a larger genie appears who empowers Aladdin to stop his mother from selling the lamp.[4]

Aladdin represents a striving young consciousness that seeks to learn about the power of communication with the forces of the invisible world. Similar stories with phrases like *abracadabra* and *open sesame* represent the power of the spoken word to manifest future dreams in the visible world. The magic lamp is a symbol of the unconscious mind illumined by a genie, which has been living within the underground garden, representing the "genius" of the unconscious. The lamp suggests the awakening power of the imagination that will help provide solutions to future problems. Within "imagination" lies the word *magi*, derived from a Persian word meaning "seer" or "wizard." It is the magi within that will help you to imagine and manifest a positive outcome in the future.

---

[4] *Inner Child Cards*, 45–47.

If you decide to work with this story, consider words that are empowering to you. Now contrast them with words that take away your voice. Notice the effect that negative words have on your body, such as slumped shoulders, shallow breathing, or a tight throat. In the space below, reflect on how you can transform these effects.

_____

_____

_____

_____

_____

Altar

As with the fourth cycle, my fifth cycle altar is the dining room table on the main level of my house. At Lughnasadh/Lammas, I change the green tablecloth to a blue one and adorn it with light-blue candles. In gratitude for the bountiful harvest that Lammas represents, I display a picture of a cornucopia brimming with fruits, vegetables, and flowers. A glass decoration with a lotus inside reminds me to allow my throat chakra to flower, and a sky-blue sapphire reminds me to expand the space around my voice before I speak. A musical symbol entices me to chant or sing to nature so that I can attune my sound to the wisdom of the natural world.

Affirmations

1) My integrity lies in seeking the truth.
2) I express my truth creatively and effectively.
3) I respond to the sound of my soul.
4) Communication is vital to my well-being.
5) My fifth chakra is filled with spirit-permeated blue light.
6) _____
7) _____
8) _____
9) _____
10) _____

CHAPTER SEVEN

PERCEIVING WITH SOUL

Cycle: Beginning on September 21 and ending on November 1, the sixth cycle is ushered in by the autumn equinox, when day and night are equal and in balance. It is a "yin" time of year, providing an opportunity to gaze inward for a life review. As you review your life, consider these questions: Are you stuck in the rut of doing the same old thing year after year? Are you feeling stressed out and overworked? Do you need a new direction on your spiritual path? This chapter asks you to look at your life from another perspective so that you can discern what needs balancing or changing.

During this cycle, you might conduct an interview with an older friend or member of your family. Perhaps he or she can help shift the way you regard growing older. Since Western culture values youthful energy over wisdom and experience, aging has fallen into shadow material. Connecting with elders can help to bring that shadow into consciousness so that you can glean the gold and view aging in a more positive light.

Celtic: The Celts called the autumn equinox *Mabon*, meaning "Son of Light." Both Mabon and his mother, Modron, come from Annwyn, the Celtic name for the Underworld. Although these names sound unfamiliar and foreign to us, we can give them relevance by relating them to our personal lives. For example, my first child was born on September 22 around the time of the autumn equinox. While my son Dan is grateful that I didn't name him Mabon and I'm just as glad not to be called Modron, you could say that we are all mothers of Mabon, or a "Son" of the light of the soul that is guiding us to spirit.

Annwyn also relates to my personal life, since "Ann" is my given name and "wyn" is often a part of names in Scotland County where I grew up. In fact, Gwynne is the first name of one of my childhood friends and the last name of one of my childhood classmates. On an archetypal level, Annwyn can be likened to the collective unconscious where the true self is rooted like a rhizome, a horizontal underground plant capable of producing the shoot-and-root systems of a new plant. Annwyn, as the collective unconscious, is a place of "underground growth," where the masculine and feminine poles of the psyche are waiting to be born as differentiated opposites.

On Halloween, which comes at the end of this cycle, consider dressing up like an archetypal creature from the Underworld. Is there a character from a fairy tale attracting your attention? It could be a positive character like Snow White or a negative character like the Wicked Queen. Don't judge yourself if the Wicked Queen comes to mind; instead, try to see her in a new light. This character might have a warning for you, such as the danger of being caught in the grip of envy or jealousy.

Sixth Chakra: The sixth chakra, also called the third eye, is located in the area between the eyebrows. Some sources say that the sixth chakra is connected to the pineal gland in the back of the brain. The pineal gland is a light-sensitive organ that, when activated, connects us to the realm of spirit. Other sources say that the sixth chakra is connected to the pituitary gland in the center of the brain. The pituitary gland is the "queen" of the endocrine system to which the chakras are psychically connected. I prefer to view the sixth chakra as connected to both the pineal and the pituitary glands, for it is at the level of the sixth chakra that spirit "marries" soul.

The color of the sixth chakra is dark blue or indigo. As the blue sky of day darkens to the indigo of night, it becomes the color of dreams and can even evoke the concept of death. Conscious thought yields little by little to the unconscious, just as the light of day gradually becomes a dark midnight blue. For Tibetan Buddhists, dark blue is the color of transcendent potentiality and emptiness, suggesting the invisible realm.[1]

What else do you associate with dark blue? Dye from the indigo plant? An indigo bunting bird? Cobalt blue? Ink? An eggplant? Blueberries? As you cloak yourself in dark blue, choose an indigo image and write down your associations.

_____

_____

_____

_____

_____

---

[1]   *Dictionary of Symbols*, 102–103.

Like dark blue, the sixth chakra has a mysterious and mystical quality. To strengthen the intuitive and psychic powers of this chakra, try dancing under the harvest moon, holding your attention on the area between your eyebrows. If dancing doesn't appeal to you, you can sketch the harvest moon or dialogue with it, again holding your attention in the area between the eyebrows. As the third eye begins to open, you may feel as though you are living with one foot in the physical body and one foot in the "imaginal body," a level of consciousness that holds the tension between instinct and image, matter and spirit.

Mentioned in the last chapter as a meditative symbol, the lotus flower can be an image of the imaginal body. With its roots firmly planted in the "mud" of daily life, its stem flowing up the waters of the unconscious, and its blossom opening to the sun of consciousness, the lotus symbolizes the intersection of the personal and the archetypal. The meeting of the personal and the archetypal signifies an inner marriage of masculine spirit and feminine soul that enables us to perceive images like the lotus as meaningful to our lives.

Beatles star John Lennon captured the essence of the imaginal body with his classic song "Imagine." In the 1960s when Lennon launched his singing career, raising consciousness was sometimes attempted through the false light of taking drugs, drinking excessive amounts of alcohol, and engaging in "free love," but the feminine was still lost. When we understand that our life force and the earth's life force are interconnected, we undergo a shift in consciousness. At this level, we may be called to participate in the intuitive and expressive arts—healing, music, art, and dance—or it may be that we're building a bridge between the ego and the true self to manifest a world enchanted with soul. In this way, the feminine becomes conscious.

It is the conscious feminine that brings the soul realm into everyday life. When the soul lives within us, it releases the creative child who loves to play, as well as the artist whose perception bridges the timeless world through imagery. Many people have buried their soulful imaginations—all that makes life vital and creative. The earth, too, is sending us warnings that her vital life force is breaking down. If we are to care for her, we must first embrace our own souls in our own flesh and honor the soul's beauty shining through our human form.[2]

The sixth chakra helps to bring the light of the feminine soul into the world in order to spiritualize—or bring consciousness to—the body and the earth. In so doing, we yield to the evolutionary power of love. It is not easy to embody the evolutionary love power that is

---

[2]   *Dancing in the Flames*, 169, and *The Maiden King*, 222.

pouring into the planet right now, but rituals can strengthen our bodies and help us to have faith in what is trying to be born.

Ritual for the Sixth Cycle

1) <u>Third Eye Meditation</u>: At the autumn equinox, the Wheel of the Year turns from outward yang activity to inward yin reflection. For this meditation, enter a state of receptivity and visualize a crescent moon shaped like a cup or grail about an inch behind the center of your eyebrows. It is surrounded by an indigo blue, like the night sky. Now imagine that the crescent moon as cup or grail is opening to a waterfall. Fill the cup completely as you purify your third eye and shift your consciousness inward. If you suffer from insomnia, try this meditation just before going to bed to relax an overactive mind.

2) <u>Active Imagination Dialogue with a Spirit Animal</u>: My spirit animal for the sixth cycle is Owl, a nocturnal bird that can see in the dark and turn its head in all directions. Owl, whose medicine is "Deception," can see that which is not readily apparent.

Me: Hello, Owl. I've heard that you are the symbol of wisdom. Is that why you've been hooting at me lately?

Owl: Whooo, me?

Me: Yes, youooo. Now what wisdom are you trying to impart?

Owl: Do you have the eyes to see? I can see in the dark, you know.

Me: Yes, I know, and you can also turn your head from side to side. Why do you do that?

Owl: So that I can look with "soft seeing."

Me: What do you mean by soft seeing?

Owl: Squint your eyes and look through them with blurred vision. This exercise will strengthen your third eye so that you see behind you, around you, and within you.

Me: How can I see within me?

Owl: Do you remember the long steps that descended into Bat Cave when you went to the mountains a few years ago?

Me: Oh my, yes. Those steps went down forever. I thought I was going straight to hell.

Owl: Well, in a way, you were. Descending into the unconscious can feel like going to hell because you see some things about yourself that you may not want to face—or about other people that you'd rather not know.

Me: Okay, if you say so, but I'd rather talk about how to do this. I suppose I could visualize myself going down those steps until I find some freedom from intrusive thoughts.

Owl: That's a good start. What happens when you're free from intrusive thoughts?

Me: I feel a kind of surrender—a letting go of the ego, I guess you could say.

Owl: Yes, the ego will be the first to deceive you. Sometimes it will tell you what you'd like to hear but not necessarily what you need to hear, and at other times, it will be your most severe inner critic.

Me: In other words, the ego can distort the truth.

Owl: It also covers up the truth. But trust me—it won't surrender without a struggle. It likes power and control, and it will want to dominate.

Me: How can I keep the ego from dominating?

Owl: Picture the ego with wings, and tell it to fly away for now. Let it know it can come back later but it is not in charge.

Me: What if I do bring up some unpleasant truths? What can I do with them?

Owl: Turn your head toward your inner self and ask what you are in the dark about.

Me: Thank you, Owl. Do you have any other words of wisdom for me?

Owl: Befriend the darkness within, and you will find the truth that sets you free.

In the spirit of Owl, try to spend as much time in nature as possible. Notice details all around the natural world. Observe the perfection and intricacies of the plants and flowers. Now imagine that you can see with the back of your head, as if you can see what is behind you, and that you are able to look with a 360-degree radius all around. For practice in receiving, imagine that the plants and flowers can look back at you. Receive them looking at you, and then gently look back at them. Have an open exchange between you and nature with no separation. Part of Owl wisdom is that we are becoming co-creators with the natural world and that it can inform us in discerning our true spiritual path.

Owl wisdom can also help you to visualize a desired outcome. For example, if you are trying to sell a house, visualize Sold on the For Sale sign in your yard. Experience the joy and relief you feel when the house is sold. Combining visualization with authentic feelings will give you a better chance of manifesting your needs in the physical world. Another example is to visualize good health, whether or not you are actually experiencing it. Since dark blue is a cool color with a high frequency, it is said to be particularly effective in treating inflammation. If you have trouble with your sinuses, for example, visualize deep blue permeating the inflamed area.

3) <u>Fairy Tale or Story</u>: Revisit a fairy tale or story from an earlier cycle and reframe it from a higher perspective. I chose to revisit "Jack and the Beanstalk" from the fourth cycle.

Plot Summary: In this adaptation of the story, let us imagine that Jack is suspended from the beanstalk headfirst. This reversed position mirrors that of a baby as it emerges from the womb or of a bat hanging upside down in a dark cave. In the reversed position, Jack is symbolically letting go of his comfortable life of status and possessions in order to move to a life of inner clarity. By going down the beanstalk headfirst, Jack is sacrificing his intellect to yield to a greater truth. He makes a blind leap into the dark, as he hangs between his old self and the new self he is becoming. Jack is on the verge of rebirth, standing at a threshold. Once he crosses the threshold, the journey toward rebirth nears its destination.[3]

On one level, this approach to "Jack and the Beanstalk" is asking us to look at our attitude toward control. Loss of control can be very frightening, but control can prevent our growth: we may be missing out on the excitement of experiencing the unknown and the opportunity to discover new things. Sometimes we just need to relax and allow events to take their course even if they seem to be the reverse of what we expected.

On another level, this story is asking us to go beyond dualistic thinking. For example, we tend to view the Mother as having two opposing aspects: the negative mother as manipulative and materialistic, like Jack's mother in this story, and the positive mother as nurturing and abundant, like the fairy godmother in "Cinderella." But they are actually flip sides of the same coin. We can't simply get rid of the negative mother and keep the positive, or else the negative will split off and become shadow material. Relating to both sides of the Mother gives us clarity about ourselves, even if we have to admit to behaving like the Wicked Queen at times!

The same applies to the Father. We may think of the negative father as someone who wants to dominate, as many of us have experienced in the Western culture, and the positive father as a dynamic leader we may have admired. Again, relating to both the negative and positive sides of the Father, rather than trying to split off the negative, is the key to holistic thinking.

A healthy sixth chakra invites us to view life from a higher state of consciousness. We begin to see life with soul perception, allowing global events to enlighten us as to what we need to look at within ourselves. When we are threatened with terrorist attacks, for example, we can

---

[3]   *Inner Child Cards*, 90–91.

look at our "inner terrorist" so that we face our own fears about making constructive changes in our lives. The sixth chakra sees with the eye of the soul, holding the tension of ambiguity and paradox.

Altar

On the autumn equinox, I set up my altar on the third level of my house, which has the feel of being in an owl's nest. My altar is adorned with a dark-blue cloth and indigo candles. Displayed are acorns, gourds, mums, and other reminders of the season. Images of owls, squirrels, cardinals, and blue jays depict the wisdom of instinctual creatures, and a lapis lazuli gemstone evokes the potentiality of the invisible world.

Affirmations

1) I open my eyes to deeper wisdom.
2) I visualize needed changes in my life.
3) I seek clarity of insight.
4) I strive to understand opposing viewpoints.
5) My sixth chakra is filled with spirit-permeated indigo light.
6) _____
7) _____
8) _____
9) _____
10) _____

CHAPTER EIGHT

EXPANDING THE IMAGINATION

Cycle: During the seventh cycle, which spans from November 1 to December 21, try cultivating thoughts of gratitude, especially at Thanksgiving on the fourth Thursday in November. This is a good time of year to start a gratitude journal, a dream journal, or any other kind of journal. Since the days are growing shorter and colder, there is more inside time for developing a spiritual practice, such as sitting quietly in meditation and detaching from everyday concerns. This chapter focuses on the spiritual practice of transcending the usual way you experience your life through expanding the imagination.

Celtic: On the Celtic Wheel of the Year, this cycle is ushered in by the celebration of Samhain (pronounced "Sow-en"). All Souls' Day on November 1 and All Saints' Day on November 2, as well as the Mexican Day of the Dead are all related to Samhain, for this is the time of year that the veil between the visible and invisible worlds is thin. In the ancient celebrations of Samhain, it was believed that humans could perceive beyond the veil between the worlds to communicate with those who had died. Bonfires guarded against any evil powers thought to be associated with the deceased and the invisible world. When supernatural powers showed up in a human being, he or she was thrown into a bonfire to ward off the perceived evil.[1]

At Samhain, one could catch sight of the shape of things to come in the womb of future time. To tune in to this "second sight," the Celts practiced the art of divination, a practice that was an aid to perceptual intuition. One potent divination tool was the hazelnut. The hazel was the magic tree that wizards loved, containing "in a nutshell" all insight and wisdom. Gathering hazelnuts at Samhain was a tradition from the Isle of Skye off the coast of Scotland. Every Samhain on the Isle of Skye, the hazelnuts ripened to scarlet and dropped from the bough

---

[1]   *The Magickal Year*, 198–200.

into the waiting mouth of the Salmon of Knowledge who then had an understanding of the invisible world.[2]

Along with the hazelnut, the apple was another divination tool. Apple bobbing, a game often played during this time of the year, is a relic of the belief that in obtaining the sacred apple, one had the ability to foresee the future and gain knowledge of the invisible world. In apple bobbing, the water is stirred with a stick or some other equivalent of a wand to keep the apple in constant motion. If a player is successful in gaining possession of the apple, then he or she can eat it—and thus acquire the power of foresight. When an apple is cut horizontally, it reveals a pentagram or a five-pointed pattern called the "Star of Knowledge." Four of the points represent the elements—water, fire, earth, and air—while the fifth point represents ether. From ether, the most subtle and pure substance, it is said that the stars were formed.[3]

Seventh Chakra: The seventh chakra, generally known as the crown chakra, is located at the top of the head. This chakra is sometimes connected to the pineal gland and at other times to the pituitary gland, depending on the source. Whether it is connected to the pineal or the pituitary, the purpose of the seventh chakra is to open us to inspired imagination and higher perceptions.

The "astral body" is associated with the starry realm of the crown chakra, as the word *astral* means "star." It is said that the chakras are organs of the astral body because the chakras link us to the ethereal plane of the stars as well as to the dense plane of earth. When you dream, the astral body can travel to either the higher or the lower planes to receive dream images. On the lower astral plane, you might have horrifying nightmares (reminiscent of Halloween spooks), and on the higher plane, you might receive messages from your guardian angel and spirit guides. The key is to work with the astral body for your soul's highest good.

To work symbolically with the higher astral body of the crown chakra, you might use the image of an amethyst radiating rays to attract divine insight. Imagine that you are wearing the amethyst as a crown, with each point of the amethyst acting as an antenna reaching toward the Divine. Since the lotus flower is often a symbol of the chakras, you could also think of the crown chakra as a "thousand-petal lotus" opening to the light of the cosmos. Whatever image you choose, be sure to ground yourself in everyday life so that there is a correspondence

---

[2] *The Magickal Year*, 209.
[3] *The Magickal Year*, 210.

between the earth plane and the heavenly plane. The saying "As above, so below" can serve as a mantra when working with this chakra.

The color of the seventh chakra is violet, the highest frequency in the rainbow spectrum. Composed of equal parts of red and blue, violet is the color of moderation and temperance since within violet the blaze of red is softened. Violet is said to be the color of secrecy, as behind it the invisible mystery of transformation takes place. Widely recognized as a spiritual color, violet represents energy flowing between heaven and earth.[4]

What else do you associate with violet? "Roses are red, violets are blue"? A shade of purple or lavender? Ultraviolet light? Consider what spiritual meaning violet has for you, and write your associations in the space below.

_____

_____

_____

_____

_____

During this cycle, many spiritual traditions are preparing to celebrate "the coming of the light." Consider, for example, the Hebrew celebration of Hanukkah with its candelabra of subtle light, and the Christian observance of Advent with its pink and purple candles. Instead of participating in rampant materialism this time of year, consider spending the first three weeks of December preparing for the coming of the light within you.

The importance of preparation was brought home to me when my second son, Greg, was born. He was due in mid-December, and given my relative youth, I thought I would have plenty of time to finish my holiday errands before he came. Instead, I had no choice but to conserve my energy and lie in wait. This experience taught me the true meaning of Advent as a time of waiting and expectation on the spiritual journey.

Many people today seem to be waiting for the light of a new awakening consciousness. Collectively, we are in an incubation period as we release the outdated energies of the Old Mother and the Old Father, those archaic parental complexes that hinder growth. We are in the process of integrating profound changes taking place in our souls and bodies as psychic

---

[4]   *Dictionary of Symbols*, 1068–1069.

energy attempts to flow between instinct and spirit. In describing this flow of energy between instinct and spirit, Jung used the image of the rainbow, asserting that everything that is alive in the psyche shimmers in rainbow hues. At the infrared pole of the spectrum is matter and instinct while at the ultraviolet pole lies the dynamism of spirit and symbols.[5]

Balancing matter and spirit requires a container that allows the light of the new awakening consciousness to grow in our relationships, in our creativity, and in our very cells. The ritual for the seventh cycle is a good way to ground this transformative light.

Ritual for the Seventh Cycle

1) <u>Star Meditation</u>: Envision your physical body as a five-pointed star, with your legs as the two lower points, your arms as the two side points, and your head as the top point. See your entire body radiating with glowing starlight. Now imagine the starlight purifying your emotional body. Then direct the starlight into the mental body, clearing your mind and thoughts. As you continue moving your consciousness through the planes of the astral body, imagine your aura expanding all over the earth, filling it with divine starlight.

2) <u>Active Imagination Dialogue with a Spirit Animal</u>: My spirit animal for the seventh cycle is Hawk. With his medicine of "Message," Hawk can send us communication from the astral planes. He sees both the big picture of the heavenly plane and the small details of the earthly plane: as he circles the vastness of the skies, he also looks down to spot his prey.

Me: Hello, Hawk. I'll bet you have all kinds of messages for me today.
Hawk: We'll see. Let's start with what's on your mind right now.
Me: I guess I'm wondering why you carry your prey around in your talons.
Hawk: The better to eat it with, my dear.
Me: Doesn't it bother you that your prey is still alive and kicking?
Hawk: Not particularly. We all have to eat, don't we?
Me: Yes, but it seems that all you do is fly around looking for prey. Why don't you do something better with your time?
Hawk: Like what?

---

[5]   *Dancing in the Flames*, 181–182.

Me: It must be fun to fly high in the skies with your mighty wingspan. If I could do that, I'd be in seventh heaven.

Hawk: Frankly, I'd rather be looking around for a good dinner. But let's talk about my wings since they seem to be on your mind. What's up with that?

Me: Maybe I wish I could fly.

Hawk: What makes you think you can't fly? Have you ever tried?

Me: Do I look like I have wings? Get real!

Hawk: Why do you think you need wings? Haven't you felt as though you are flying when you're doing something you really enjoy? What about the times your writing is going really well and you're on a creative high? To fly, all you need is your imagination.

Me: Oh, I'd probably just imagine that something awful is about to happen, or I'd dismiss it as a flight of fantasy.

Hawk: Can you imagine clouds?

Me: Sure—white and fluffy, nestled in an azure sky, or gray and threatening, full of rain. Or spread thin over the horizon mixed with purple and pink in a glorious sunset.

Hawk: Very good! Now imagine that you have my wings and you're flying over and around the clouds. Can you do that?

Me: Yes, but is this really flying?

Hawk: There you go again with your "Yes, buts." Do you believe that what you see and hear and touch are the only realities?

Me: Well, aren't they?

Hawk: Try soaring away from your usual way of perceiving and trust the signals that you're receiving.

Me: Oh, so now you're a poet.

Hawk: Being a poet takes imagination. Now start perceiving with yours.

Me: Okay, here goes. I see another reality in another time and place. There's a garden with lush flowers and ferns. In the center of the garden is a tree with gnarly roots reaching down into the center of the earth and branches reaching high into the heavens.

Hawk: Yes, that's the Tree of Life. We'll get to that later, but for now, I want you to imagine yourself in my body with my wingspan.

Me: You're making me a little nervous, me in your body and all that.

Hawk: Don't worry—I'll come get you if you're frightened.

Me: I hope you won't come get me in your talons. I don't want to be your lunch!

Hawk: I'll keep a keen eye on you and zero in if you get into trouble.

Me: So you are my protector of sorts.

Hawk: Yes, I'm your father-protector within. You're safe with me.

Me: Thank you, Hawk, but do you have anything else to say?

Hawk: Let's go back to the Tree of Life in the garden. Now turn it upside down so that its roots reach up into the Milky Way and its branches go down into the earth. There you will find a message about being rooted in heaven while blooming on earth.

In the spirit of Hawk, find time during this cycle to walk in the mountains. If this isn't possible, use your imagination. As you ascend to the top of the mountain, view your life from a higher perspective. As you descend the mountain, tune into the mundane details. How do the details of your life fit into the bigger picture of your spiritual journey?

Hawk is akin to Mercury, the Roman messenger of the gods. His cry signals the need to heighten your awareness about the magic of life. Hawk is asking you to question your habitual thought patterns so that a new pattern can take its place. Record your insights in a journal to connect the dots of your life and to discern their meaning for your spiritual path.

3) <u>Fairy Tale or Story:</u> This cycle offers a good opportunity for you to create your own story. Here's a possible title and scenario: "The Cosmic Earth Child," a story about a soul with the potential for multidimensional consciousness. By learning difficult lessons on earth, as well as joyful ones, the human soul begins to comprehend the vast scope of existence in the infinite universe. The beauty, majesty, and complexity of life on earth are woven together within the fabric of this Cosmic Earth Child, who makes a conscious choice to reenter the physical world and once again take up the challenge of earthly living.[6]

Now imagine that you are this Cosmic Earth Child. As you experience universal harmony emanating from the sun, notice the rhythmic beating of your heart, the radiant sun center within your body. Visualize the cosmic wisdom encoded in your DNA and in your cellular memory. Now bring this wisdom to the crown chakra and tune into the cosmos. What insights does the heavenly realm reveal to you about your spiritual direction?

Since The Cosmic Earth Child is multidimensional, it can live in the past, present, and future simultaneously. It can tap into the conscious and unconscious minds at will, as well as transcend dualistic thinking. It can dwell in the physical realm of matter and the archetypal realm of the gods. You are the midwife for this child. What can you do to help birth it? Once it

---

[6] *Inner Child Cards*, 127–128.

is born, how will it live its life on earth? How can it serve humanity by returning to the earth plane? Let your imagination run freely as the story unfolds.

_____

_____

_____

_____

_____

Altar

As with the sixth cycle, my seventh cycle altar is in the uppermost area of my house. This room has a skylight that lets in the higher frequencies of the crown chakra. I place a light-purple cloth on my altar and adorn it with violet candles along with an amethyst gemstone. A picture of a rainbow conveys the link between heaven and earth, and a gold pot holds the treasures at the end of the rainbow. A picture of Hawk serves as a reminder that the details of my life are pointing toward a higher meaning.

Affirmations

1) My astral body links the lower and higher planes.
2) The cosmos supports me.
3) My soul is eternal.
4) I trust that my highest good is unfolding.
5) My seventh chakra is filled with spirit-permeated violet light.
6) _____
7) _____
8) _____
9) _____
10) _____

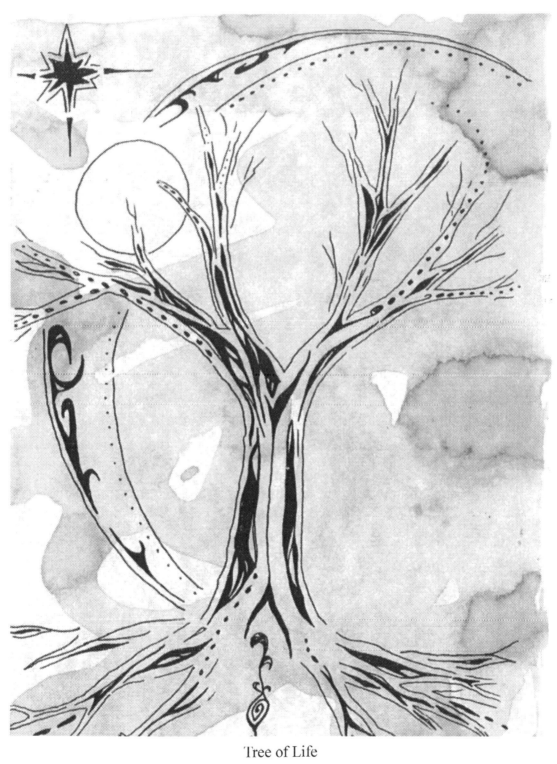

Tree of Life

CHAPTER NINE

LIGHTING THE PATH

Cycle: Beginning on December 21 and ending on January 6, the eighth cycle is a sacred period of time in most religious traditions. While some people may have an adverse reaction to the word *religious* and prefer to say that they are "spiritual," it is important to keep in mind that "religion" is related to the Latin root *ligare*, meaning "to link," as suggested by the word *ligament*. So that religion doesn't fall into shadow material, this chapter explores ways to make space for the religious instinct, as we focus on the soul as a link between heaven and earth.

This cycle begins with the solstice, a word meaning "sun stands still." As the shortest day of the year, the winter solstice may indeed seem like a time when the sun is standing still and frozen in the sky, yielding little light. Just as the light begins to emerge from the darkness at the solstice season, there is also a weaving of the dark and light within the soul.

Celtic: During the time of the winter solstice, the Celts celebrated Yule. *Yule* is derived from the Scandinavian word for *wheel*. The burning of the Yule log was an important ritual in the turning of the Wheel of the Year toward the light. Fire was the sun's representative on earth, seen as a life-giving force to lighten the darkness. The log itself was venerated because it represented the Green Man, the vegetation deity whose ashes were thought to have magical, fertilizing powers. The Celts believed that keeping a piece of the Yule log throughout the year ensured plentiful crops, helped cattle to breed easily, protected against lightning, and held promise that the light would return.[1]

Eighth Chakra: A spinning vortex located several inches over the head, the eighth chakra is transcendental in nature, meaning that it goes beyond the limitations of the light spectrum. Notice that when the number eight is turned on its side, it resembles the infinity sign. Perhaps

---

[1]   *The Magickal Year*, 39–41.

humanity is becoming more aware of the eighth chakra as we develop cosmic consciousness and awaken to the soul's link to infinity.

While most midwinter celebrations abound with strings of outer light, the eighth chakra calls us to attune to the light within and release it from the darkness. As you work (and play) with the eighth chakra, your "light body" is evolving, becoming, and growing out of the darkness into the light of consciousness.

In addition to the meaning of "to brighten" and as the opposite of dark, the word *light* has various other connotations: information, consciousness, illumination, energy, truth, and insight. You can probably think of several other ways to describe "light." The term *lightworker* has entered into our collective lexicon today, referring to those who are bringing light to humanity in some way. Ways of bringing light to humanity can range from imparting wisdom and information to clearing blocked energy, exploring higher consciousness, working for social justice, and relating to the light spectrum as we are doing in this book.

The "color" for the eighth chakra is white, the sum of all the colors on the light spectrum. White represents east and west, the two points at which the sun is born and dies each day. Possessing the properties of a boundary, as in the horizon, white acts upon our souls like a silence that is not lifeless but replete with potential. The color of mother's milk, white points to something that nourishes that potential. White sometimes takes the form of a halo over the head, indicating enlightenment.[2]

What else do you associate with white? A snowflake? A lily or a lotus? Clouds? Santa's beard? A bridal gown? The north pole? As you immerse yourself in the purity of white, explore some other images in the space below.

_____

_____

_____

_____

_____

As you go through this cycle, pay attention to images of white light in the natural world. All you have to do is look up at the sky this time of year, and you will get a sense of the ethereal

---

[2]   *Dictionary of Symbols*, 105.

quality of light dancing within silvery white clouds. The star is a powerful image of this living light, reminding us that we are made of stardust and that our own sun is a star. A symbol of hope, the star is a beacon of white light shining out of the surrounding darkness of the night sky.

With his white beard and suit trimmed in white, Santa Claus is a central image in the Christian religion this time of year. Santa is said to have been based on St. Nicholas, a fourth-century bishop who was the model of propriety and virtue. But Santa has a whole team of helpers of pre-Christian lineage, such as elves and reindeer. Gliding across the sky with a team of reindeer amid the jangle of elfin bells, Santa conjures up a picture of the shaman riding the crest of the universe to bestow gifts from the Otherworld. Sliding down the chimney with a sack on his back, Santa mirrors the shaman climbing down the World Tree to bring healing gifts to the community.[3]

The Virgin Mary giving birth to the divine child is also an image coming from Christianity, but as an archetype, the virgin transcends all traditions. Like the virgin forest that carries the potential of new life, within the virgin is contained the seed of a new consciousness. When nurtured, this seed matures into a transformative light that can hold the tension between soul and spirit. The virgin, an aspect of the soul that is inwardly present as creative receptivity, hears and sees with eternal ears and eyes, resonating with a dimension beyond time and space.[4]

As you turn the page to a new year, a good image to meditate upon is Father Time. Notice that when you reverse the letters in "time," you get "emit." During this cycle, imagine that you are emitting strands of the light body by weaving white light throughout the corners of the earth. In this way, you are psychically repairing the web of creation, which has been frayed through years of pollution, bombs, global warming, and negative thought forms.

No matter what religious tradition we prefer, the eighth cycle is a profoundly spiritual spoke on the Wheel of the Year. In performing the ritual for this cycle, we honor the light of the soul in the "earth" of our own bodies.

---

[3] *The Magickal Year*, 52–56.
[4] *Dancing in the Flames*, 185–186.

Ritual for the Eighth Cycle

1) <u>Light Meditation</u>: Visualize a halo over your head, brimming with vibrant white light. As you attune to this halo, bring the white light into the center of your brain. Allow the light to circulate throughout your brain, and then slowly bring your focus back to the halo shining over your head. This meditation can help you to transcend the cerebral intellect in order to make space for inspirational messages coming from the higher realms. If you suffer from seasonal affective disorder (SAD) or if the holidays are stressful, you will find this meditation particularly healing and uplifting.

2) <u>Active Imagination Dialogue with a Spirit Animal</u>: My spirit animal for the eighth cycle is Crow. With the medicine of sacred "Law," Crow honors the dark and light in all of creation, as well as both inner and outer reality. Like the eighth chakra, Crow's Law takes us beyond our habitual way of thinking.

Me: Hello, Crow. Lately, I've noticed that you and your "crow-nies" have been gathering in my front yard. Can you tell me what that's about?

Crow: Have you also noticed a lot of squawking when you're out walking?

Me: Yes, sometimes I say to myself that the crows surely are loud today.

Crow: Well, then, it seems I am trying to get your attention, doesn't it?

Me: Okay, what is it that you're trying to tell me?

Crow: If you want a direct answer, you should know that's not my law.

Me: I can tell right now that this is not going to be an easy conversation.

Crow: My law isn't about easy conversations. Crow is a bird of a different color.

Me: Yes, and that color is black—not my favorite, to be honest.

Crow: What is it about black that bothers you?

Me: Now please don't take offense—it's just that I like bright colors, ones that are full of hope and optimism.

Crow: It appears that black is a shadow color for you. What's in that shadow message?

Me: Maybe darkness conjures up images of depression, like going into a black hole. That's something to avoid if you ask me.

Crow: Depression could be a symptom of the need for some kind of change in your life. My law signifies change on many levels.

Me: Are you trying to tell me that I resist change?

Crow: I'm saying that you tend to be a pain avoider. Change can bring pain, you know.

Me: You're right. I'd have to be pretty desperate to change the present if it feels comfortable. And truth to tell, I'm not feeling at all comfortable with this conversation.

Crow: Okay, I'll come back another day when you're ready for my mystery.

Me: That's it? You're leaving?

Crow: Yes, for now, but give me a "caw" when you get a chance.

Me: I don't mean to be rude, Crow, but frankly, you're starting to feel a little spooky.

Crow: Speaking of spook, do you remember that Halloween costume you made a few years ago? You glued bird feathers on your son's black graduation gown and even decorated a hat to match.

Me: Yes, that costume was something of an inspiration, if I do say so myself. I glued beads down the front of the gown and on the top of the hat to represent the chakras.

Crow: What inspired you to glue chakra beads on your costume?

Me: The chakras are power centers, and the beads represent my inner power.

Crow: The power to do what?

Me: Hmmm … maybe the power to be a shaman. Thank you, Crow, for visiting me today. Is there something else you'd like to add?

Crow: Well, at least you got the part about the shaman—now meditate on the chakras. The message may come when you see me gathering again in your front yard or squawking overhead or even appearing in a dream.

In the spirit of Crow, imagine a source filled with vast energy at the galactic center of the Milky Way. Now envision all the chakra colors in a prism embedded in this source. As the colors emerge and stream from the prism, visualize your chakras being lit up one by one like bulbs on a Christmas tree: red for the first chakra, orange for the second, yellow for the third, green for the fourth, blue for the fifth, indigo for the sixth, and violet for the seventh. In this way, you become like the World Tree, a symbolic link between heaven and earth.

As a shamanic bird, Crow can navigate the realm of dreams to help you discern and release the light in the darkness. One night during a particularly stressful holiday season, I dreamed that I was walking with my deceased cat, Lily, in an unfamiliar area. Lily was standing on her hind legs with one paw in my hand, as a human would walk. Turning a corner, Lily and I spotted colorful markets along the sidewalks, and then someone familiar appeared with a big smile on his face. I recognized him as a friend from Carolina Health and Humor Association, an organization that works with hospitals and charities to bring the healing light of humor to situations that could be perceived as dark and humorless.

The next morning, as I recorded this dream in my journal, I "cawed" on the wisdom of Crow, and he offered this interpretation: Walking upright like a human, Lily represents an aspect of my instinctual nature coming into the light of consciousness. In this situation, Lily is leading me to my innate sense of humor, which usually gets me through stressful times. The colorful markets and my friend from the humor organization represent the need to lighten up and change my perspective on holiday chores. As I worked with this dream, time seemed to stand still to allow space for me to finish up all that I needed to do. Perhaps Crow was illustrating an aspect of his law: that time is relative, depending on our attitude.

3) <u>Fairy Tale or Story:</u> My fairy tale for this ritual is "Rapunzel," a story that captures the essence of the soul's journey on the path to wholeness.

Plot Summary: In the story, a couple prays for a child. Their wish is granted when the woman gives birth to a daughter, whom they name "Rapunzel." One day, the woman asks her husband to go next door to an enchantress's garden to get some herbs to heal their ailing young daughter. The enchantress tells the husband that if he wants the herbs, he must hand over his daughter at puberty. The husband agrees, and when Rapunzel reaches her twelfth birthday, the enchantress takes her away and locks her in a tower without steps.

One day, a prince hears Rapunzel singing, and he watches as the enchantress calls on Rapunzel to let down her braid. When he sees that the enchantress has left the tower, the prince calls out, "Rapunzel! Rapunzel! Let down your hair." The enchantress soon discovers that Rapunzel has been visited by the prince, so she cuts off Rapunzel's braid, abandons her in a desert, and takes Rapunzel's place in the tower. When the prince returns, the enchantress lets down the braid and then cuts it in half, causing the prince to fall and lose his sight. While wandering around blind, the prince meets Rapunzel in the desert. Her tears heal his vision, and they live happily ever after with their twins, a boy and a girl.[5]

The tower can symbolize the ego's guardedness and defensiveness, and the enchantress can represent the negative mother that locks up Rapunzel's blossoming creativity. Rapunzel's long hair represents the power of intuition over the ego's narrow way of looking at the world. Her singing emphasizes the need for her voice to be recognized by the outside world, while the blinded prince is a warning against the masculine tendency to become too dependent on

---

[5]   *Inner Child Cards*, 107–108.

outer sight. The newborn twins stand for the masculine and feminine poles of the psyche, once enmeshed in the womb of the second chakra and now birthed as equal partners.

If you interact with "Rapunzel," tune into the voice in the depths of the unconscious. What do you hear? What "tower" is keeping you from finding your true spiritual path?

Altar

On the winter solstice, I adorn my upstairs altar with a white cloth and white candles. Cotton balls represent snowflakes, which point to the pure aspects of nature. A figure of Santa depicts a shaman who can journey between the visible and invisible worlds. Images of angels beckon me to turn to the "higher angels of my nature" when outer yang activities compete with inner yin energies during the busy holiday season. A clear quartz crystal symbolizes the crystalline beauty that resides within the earth.

Affirmations

1) I honor both the dark and the light within creation.
2) I carry the seed of a new consciousness within my soul.
3) My light body illuminates all that surrounds me.
4) I commune with the stars.
5) My eighth chakra is filled with spirit-permeated white light.
6) _____
7) _____
8) _____
9) _____
10) _____

Winter Solstice

CHAPTER TEN

SHINING FORTH

Cycle: The ninth cycle begins on January 6 with the celebration of Epiphany and ends on February 1, where we began. *Epiphany*—a word meaning "to shine forth" or "to come to a sudden revelation"—commemorates the journey of the Magi following the star in the east to the stable where the divine child was born. While Epiphany isn't officially part of the Celtic tradition, it provides an excellent opportunity to reflect on the revelations that have come to you during the journey around the Wheel of the Year. This chapter offers guidance in synthesizing these insights as you give birth to the divine child shining forth within your soul.

Celtic: Celtic spirituality is coming back into our collective awareness, in part because it honors the light shining forth in the natural world. The Celts believed that the soul has an affinity for the natural world and that divinity is in the rivers, in the hills, and in the stones. They believed it is the soul that pierces the veil between the visible natural world and the invisible archetypal world, allowing for an exchange of energy that benefits all of creation.

Many people today are attracted to the knot that adorns Celtic art and jewelry. The strands of the knot interweave loosely and gracefully, mirroring the interdependence of the visible and invisible worlds. Carved on the base and arms of the Celtic cross, these knots reinforce the unity of the worlds.

Ninth Chakra: The ninth chakra is a metaphorical symbol for this unity consciousness. It can be imagined as an energy field that unites all the chakras into a differentiated whole. From the vantage point of unity consciousness, the star in the east from the Epiphany story represents the cosmic realm of the eighth chakra, and the stable (along with the animals) represents the instinctual grounding of the first chakra.

All of the colors of the light spectrum come together in the ninth chakra to form a "rainbow body." You might think of the rainbow body as a geometric shape shining forth around the physical body like a hologram, which is a light projection that appears translucent and multidimensional. To cite a modern example, a rainbow transmission hologram is commonly seen on credit cards for security purposes. A fractal can be another image of the rainbow body. An example of a fractal from the natural world is the growth pattern of trees, whose stems grow into smaller branches until becoming interconnected at the top.

Reflect now on what you associate with the image of the rainbow. Judy Garland singing "Over the Rainbow"? A prism? An arc in the sky as sunlight filters through raindrops? Noah's ark? Diversity, as in the Rainbow Coalition? The rainbow bridge? The colors of the DNA double helix? As you attune to the rainbow spectrum, write down your associations.

_____

_____

_____

_____

_____

The modern movie *Australia* speaks to the theme of the rainbow as a bridge between worlds or dimensions. During *Australia*, clips from the classic movie *The Wizard of Oz* are interspersed with the plot: Dorothy clicks her ruby-red slippers and repeats "There's no place like home" while an innocent Aboriginal boy sings "Over the Rainbow" to the people with whom he shares a soul connection. Through the purity of his soul, the boy is able to learn from his shaman grandfather how to be at home in the dimension of real time as well as in the dreamtime of his Aboriginal heritage.

Many of us today are split off from the multidimensional nature of the soul, and when pure soul energy begins to permeate our bodies, we may start to feel anxious. If the subtle body is not strong enough to contain this energy, we might fall into addictive behavior to quiet the anxiety: we grab for "mother" (food), "spirit" (alcohol), "divine union" (sex), or "light" (drugs) as substitutes. These addictions can lead to "soul murder," putting us in danger of regressing to "Mother Crocodile," the dark soul energy of the negative mother that mires us down in the mud, leaving us feeling criticized and uncreative.[1]

---

[1]   *Dancing in the Flames*, 189.

As noted in the last chapter, the virgin archetype contains the seed of a new soul consciousness that is attempting to birth us out of the mud into the light. Since it is during this cycle that the new soul consciousness is most likely to make itself known, watch your dreams for the appearance of a baby or a vulnerable child who requires nurturing. As the new consciousness grows and matures, it becomes "Sophia," Holy Wisdom. Sophia is a higher order of the soul that redeems the regressive energy of Mother Crocodile. The power of this new soul consciousness is "love"; the psychological state is "interdependence"; and the structure is "ecological."[2]

"Love" in this sense is an evolutionary power. If you truly love someone, you want that person to evolve his or her light potential and to live from the true self. When love is the guiding force, the psyche forms an "interdependent" relationship with all of creation, like the parts of a hologram or the growth patterns of a fractal. In this psychological state, meaningful coincidences or synchronicities come with increasing frequency, indicating that the outer and inner worlds are indeed interdependent. The structure of such a consciousness is "ecological" in that we become co-creators with nature, rather than wield our power over and against the natural world.

A challenging part of this transformational consciousness is the realization of an interiorized spirituality. It is dependent upon pulling back the projections of divinity outside of ourselves so that we can begin the process of connecting with our own divinity. In Jungian language, this new way of being is about allowing Sophia's soul wisdom to guide ego consciousness, rather than the other way around. Jung believed that the feminine soul possesses a larger measure of truth than masculine ego consciousness. Both women and men alike need to open themselves to the feminine to access their interiorized divinity, balancing the ego with the wisdom of the soul.[3]

For the ninth cycle ritual, consider a central image that serves as a balance for the ego and the soul. One possible image is a seesaw, like the ones on the playground of your childhood, with a male child on one end of the seesaw and a female child on the other. If they are to succeed in the play of the seesaw, they need to work together, neither one trying to upend the other. Inherent in the image of the seesaw is that ups and downs are a part of everyday life and that a playful attitude is important in achieving balance.

---

[2] *Dancing in the Flames*, 207.
[3] *Dancing in the Flames*, 207.

Ritual for the Ninth Cycle

1) <u>Rainbow Meditation</u>: Imagine the rainbow colors coming together to form a filament around your physical body. A deep-red hue swirls around the lower body and mingles with orange as it rises into the abdomen. Orange mixes with bright yellow in the solar plexus, and yellow flows into green in the heart center. As green moves into the area of the throat, the color turns to sky blue and then to indigo as it goes up into the area between the eyebrows. As indigo travels up into the brain cells, the color shifts to violet. A vibrant rainbow aura is now shining forth within you and around you.

2) <u>Active Imagination Dialogue with a Spirit Animal</u>: My spirit animal for the ninth cycle is Porcupine, whose medicine is "Innocence." Porcupine symbolizes the image of the divine child with its qualities of trust, creativity, and playfulness.

Me: Hello, Porcupine. I don't think I've ever seen a porcupine before. Where have you been all my life?

Porcupine: Oh, here and there, near and far, somewhere over the rainbow.

Me: That's not very helpful. Where do you live anyway?

Porcupine: I come from northern and western climes.

Me: I'm from the Southeast. You probably wouldn't feel at home where I live.

Porcupine: I don't know about that. I feel at home just about anywhere that people accept me. Trouble is, some people are put off by my sharp quills.

Me: If you're such a friendly fellow, why are you armed with those things?

Porcupine: Just because I have quills doesn't mean I'm going to use them—only when I've lost trust in the other fellow.

Me: I'm glad I don't have to carry around those unsightly things. They must do a good job of keeping people away.

Porcupine: Yeah, they do. Do you ever have that feeling?

Me: What feeling?

Porcupine: Of keeping people away because you have sent out some sharp signal.

Me: Well, sometimes I have a sharp tongue. That could keep people away all right.

Porcupine: So you've sometimes used your tongue as a quill. When does this happen?

Me: Usually when I'm feeling stressed and under pressure—and then I tend to lash out.

Porcupine: Why do you lash out at others when you are the one who is overcommitted?

Me: Maybe I'm not giving myself enough time to play. Lately, it has been work, work, and more work. All of this is weighing me down.

Porcupine: That would certainly get my quills going. I like to play.

Me: Me, too! I think I'll find something fun to do today. What do you suggest?

Porcupine: What did you like to do as a child?

Me: I played outside a lot. It was wonderful to roam in the woods and to be out in nature—just free and easy, feeling the breeze in my hair. And I used to love to shoot basketball goals with my friends. I was a natural playmate.

Porcupine: It sounds like you need to switch from setting goals to shooting goals!

Me: You're right. I'm going to find a friend to play with today. Thank you, Porcupine. Do you have another message for me before I go?

Porcupine: Your inner child is always eager to play. Let her show you the way.

Your inner child opens the imagination and gives you new ways of looking at life. I have experienced this firsthand with my six grandchildren: granddaughters Mackenzie, Olivia, Emma Rose, Caroline, Ellie, and grandson Owen. Whenever I am with them, I am often surprised by a yearning to recapture the child within myself. As I watch them swim in the dark Lumbee River of my childhood and play on the roots of the old Cypress trees, I am transported back to a more innocent time in my life when I swam with snakes and had no fear of the river's current.

To recapture the child is to nurture the soul. Our souls are like an eternal child who calls for constant care. It is the part of the personality that yearns to develop and become whole. In the spirit of Porcupine, ask what part of your soul needs more attention and care.

When I asked my soul what it needed most, the answer I received was "more fun and fantasy." In response, I treated myself to a trip to Disney World at the Magic Kingdom. As I rode on Snow White's Scary Adventure, I viewed the Wicked Queen as the negative mother, and I asked the child to help me have compassion for her. As I watched Cinderella's fairy godmother ride through the streets on a pumpkin float, I knew that I could call on the love of the positive mother as a sustaining and nurturing source for my child.

3) Fairy Tale or Story: For the ninth cycle, I chose to interact with two fairy tales that draw on the image of the child: "The Pied Piper" and "Goldilocks and the Three Bears."

Plot summary: In "The Pied Piper," the town of Hamelin finds itself infested with rats. A mysterious visitor arrives and says he will pipe the rats into the river for a fee, but after he completes the deed, the townspeople refuse to pay him. The visitor becomes angry and pipes an enchanting tune that mesmerizes the children to follow him through a door into a magic mountain. As the children follow the pied piper, one child is shut out when the door to the mountain closes. He is a wounded boy who is touched by the muse, the source of creative inspiration, but cannot find a way to manifest this power in the world.[4]

The rats suggest the negative deeds of the town leaders who won't pay the piper. They refuse to value the muse and as a result lose their future genius in the form of the children. Notice that when you reverse the word *rats*, you get *star*. If you decide to interact with this story, ask the muse to transmute the rats of scarcity and blocked creativity into your guiding star of inspiration.

In "Goldilocks and the Three Bears," we are introduced to an orderly existence of bear sizes, porridge bowls, chairs, and beds. The bears have designed a secure and fixed way of life that is disturbed by Goldilocks, who represents childlike curiosity.[5]

Plot Summary: When Goldilocks comes across the cottage of the three bears, she peers into a window and feels safe enough to go in. She tries each bear's bowl of porridge. "This one is too cold," she says, "and this one is too hot." As she tries the third one, she finds that it is "just right." Then she tries the beds. "This one is too hard, and this one is too soft," she says, but when she tries the third one, she finds that it is "just right." As the bears return from their daily travels, they ask, "Who has been eating my porridge? Who has been sleeping in my bed?" When Goldilocks hears the bears, she is frightened by their reaction and flees. The bears have chased Goldilocks away, the child who wants to experiment until she finds just the right balance.

Reflect now on how you interact with new situations and changes. How does the bears' sense of organization and order reflect your own behavior patterns and habits? Is your spiritual path too fixed and rigid? And how do you react to outsiders? Do you welcome them into your life?

_____

_____

_____

_____

_____

---

[4]   *Inner Child Cards*, 167–168.
[5]   *Inner Child Cards*, 233–234.

Altar

Like the sixth, seventh, and eighth cycles, my altar for the ninth cycle is in the uppermost area of my house. With multicolored candles and gemstones, it has the feel of a rainbow arcing through the sky. As a way of looking backward, I read insights from my journal over the past year, and as a way of looking forward, I write hopes and dreams for the New Year. My cheerful and colorful rainbow altar makes the statement that the future is full of promise.

Affirmations

1) I seek balance in all that I do.
2) I nurture my inner child.
3) A new soul consciousness is evolving within me.
4) I am in touch with my divine potential.
5) The ninth chakra fills my aura with rainbow-permeated light.
6) _____
7) _____
8) _____
9) _____
10) _____

CHAPTER ELEVEN

SPIRALING THE CYCLES

If you bring forth what is within you, what you bring forth will save you. If you do
not bring forth what is within you, what you do not bring forth will destroy you.
—The Gospel of Thomas

Now that the Wheel of the Year has come full circle and you have brought forth some
important aspects of what is within you, it is time to explore the second sentence from the
above quotation. The word *destroy* in this sentence can be intimidating and off-putting unless
we reframe it. By reframing the cycles as a spiral this time, we can delve further into the
unconscious to pick up the abandoned parts of the soul that have the potential to be destructive.
This chapter is more than just summarizing the cycles; it is about spiraling into deeper areas
of psychic growth. Throughout the chapter, I mention books that may be helpful in fostering
this new growth and in discerning a spiritual path that comes from within you.

In many ways, finding a true spiritual path parallels the individuation process. Individuation
brings forth the shadow side of the psyche into the light: the instincts are recovered and
brought into consciousness, and projections are acknowledged as messages from the true self.
As you spiral around the cycles, you allow your soul to guide you to an individuated spiritual
path. For more about individuation, I recommend Deldon Anne McNeely's book, *Becoming:
An Introduction to Jung's Concept of Individuation.*

As you revisit the cycles, you might want to continue to work with the same spirit animals
so that you can fully integrate their medicine. However, if you enjoy communicating with a
variety of animals, feel free to choose different ones. A book that works with the healing power
of animals is Dawn Baumann Brunke's *Animal Voices, Animal Guides: Discover Your Deeper*

Self through Communication with Animals. The inspirational stories and exercises in this book can help you to reclaim your instinctual and intuitive way of discerning a spiritual path.

In my own work, I have chosen to continue with the same animals. For example, my spirit animal for the first cycle is Turkey, whose Give-Away medicine offsets the ego attitude of scarcity. Given that the first chakra is about getting to the root of an issue, I recalled that in the energy field of my family, there was anxiety about whether my father could support us. When my mother returned to the workplace as a teacher, we got along pretty well financially, but the scarcity complex had already begun to form. The scarcity complex, which many of us can relate to, has the potential to destroy our ability to receive abundance.

When I was able to get to the root of scarcity, I began experimenting with giving away some of my money to worthy causes and organizations. The hold that money had on me then started to loosen, and I began to feel grateful for what I had rather than worry about what I didn't have. I also started appreciating the bounty of Mother Nature and expressing gratitude for her gifts. This opening to Mother Earth has helped me to feel less like an orphan on the planet and more like an integral part of the human family.

Healing familial and ancestral complexes is part of what the first chakra is about. Going back generations, we mindlessly repeat certain deep patterns, and revisiting the first cycle with consciousness can yield insight into these patterns. In this way, we are reaching back through a long line of ancestors to heal the strands of time. It may even be that a new archetype of time is calling to us so that our souls are more in rhythm with the seasons and the stars than with our man-made calendars. Rather than use the phrase "kill time," we can enliven the archetype of time in the collective unconscious and learn how to travel the time lines, as did the shamans.

Going back through time to connect with ancestral roots can shed light on family names. For example, in researching the origin of my maiden name, "Buie," I discovered that it means "fair-haired, peace-loving people from the Tuatha de Danann." Some sources say that the Tuatha de Danann was a mythological race forced to go underground when Ireland was taken over by neighboring tribes. Other sources mention the Tuatha de Danann as fairies or nature spirits. I am still learning about my Celtic roots and trust that just the right information will fall into my hands. One step in that direction is the work of R. J. Stewart, a scholar in the Celtic tradition. His books *Earth Light* and *Power within the Land* offer ways to work with my Celtic ancestry.

As you revisit the second cycle, the dynamics of the masculine and feminine polarities come more into play. In Jungian language, the masculine is called the "animus" (spirit) and the feminine is called the "anima" (soul). Relating to the animus provides the impulse toward consciousness and spurs us on to find our individuated path. The anima helps us to relate to the inner world of the psyche so that our path is more true and creative. If we get stuck in the second chakra, as many people do, we may remain unconscious of the dynamics of the animus and anima, and unrealistic projections in our relationships may be the result.

On the idealized side of the animus archetype, a woman may see a man as Prince Charming and expect him to make the decision about what spiritual path she should follow. On the idealized side of the anima archetype, a man may see a woman as Cinderella and expect to live happily ever after with his beautiful (and submissive) princess. When these projections inevitably fall apart, the negative side of the archetype likely kicks in: she sees him as Peter Pan, naive and ungrounded, and he sees her as the Wicked Queen, jealous and manipulative—and then they wonder what happened to the once-soulful relationship! In his book, *The Invisible Partners*, Jungian analyst John Sanford delves further into animus/anima projections.

While many of us can attest to the truth behind the animus and anima, I believe that both males and females today are having trouble relating to the anima, the part of the psyche that animates life and connects us to the instincts. (Note that *animal* comes from the same root as *anima*.) Virtual connections through technology and social networking contribute to this anima deficit and do not fulfill the need for personal contact. The *anima mundi*, or the world soul, may also be crying out through floods and tsunamis. It seems as if the water of the second chakra is spilling out in all directions with the warning that we are destroying what makes life soulful.

Spiraling into the third cycle may set in motion a strong resistance from the ego. The ego does not give up its power easily and will send up blocks wherever it can. As you attempt to loosen the grip of the ego, you will likely hear its voice getting louder and louder. Consequently, you may ignore the call of the soul by increasing the time you spend with technology or continuing to play a sport in spite of an injury (I'm speaking from experience here). This is a good time to dialogue with the fears of the ego.

Me: Hello, Fear, I haven't seen you in a while. How are you doing?
Fear: What do you mean you haven't seen me in a while? I surely have seen me in you.
Me: Where have you seen fear in me?

Fear: In your eyes, for one place. When you feel me, your eyes are like those of a deer caught in the headlights.

Me: Have I been caught in the headlights lately?

Fear: Girl, you are always caught in the headlights. Get it? Headlights! Your head is forever lit up with thoughts—and fearful ones at that.

Me: Hmmm, so you're saying that I'm an "awfulizer," as in, what if something awful happens?

Fear: Well, you are kind of a worrywart. I bet you're worrying about something right now.

Me: Yes, the IRS is in my thoughts right now. I consider it a good day when I haven't heard from them.

Fear: What are you afraid they will do?

Me: I'm afraid they'll send us a big fat letter saying we owe all kinds of money and we're being penalized with interest as long as we don't pay it. And worse—we could get audited.

Fear: Have you ever been audited?

Me: No, but my parents were audited several times. My father almost had a nervous breakdown because of an IRS audit, and my mother was very angry with him because of it. That was tense all right!

Fear: Ah, ha! So your fear of the IRS goes back to a vulnerable time in your life when you felt helpless and upset because of the home environment.

Me: By George, I think you've got it! Thank you, Fear. Is there anything else?

Fear: Notice that I rhyme with deer. Deer is a gentle creature. When you are caught in the headlights, be gentle with yourself, my dear.

Related to fear is anxiety about change or trying something new. In your family of origin, perhaps it was your mother who modeled anxiety when under pressure. Just as you might visualize fear as a restrictive father figure, like the IRS, you can visualize anxiety as a worried mother figure. Then you can dialogue with anxiety to find out the message behind it.

When you get in touch with your fear and anxiety and other feelings of vulnerability, you are on your way to spiraling into the fourth cycle. As you attune to the heart chakra, you will likely evoke Eros, the archetypal power of relatedness that weaves the parts of the psyche together like the intertwining leaves of green ivy. For reading during this cycle, I recommend William Anderson's book *The Green Man: The Archetype of Our Oneness with the Earth*. The Green Man is coming back into the collective awareness because of our feeling of separation from other realms of creation. The green leaves coming out of his mouth and head signal the greening of the imagination to communicate with these realms. At this point, you may want to dialogue with another realm, such as that of "Fairy."

Me: Hello, Fairy. What did I come to earth to heal?

Fairy: What needs to be healed in you?

Me: I'm not sure. There are probably many broken places within me.

Fairy: I like to come through the broken places. You know—through holes in trees, splits in branches, cracks in wood.

Me: Tell me, Fairy, do you have a healing elixir for my back?

Fairy: What's wrong with your back?

Me: I have a bulging disk on my lumbar 5. It pinches a nerve and hurts like the dickens.

Fairy: How did that happen?

Me: Oh, I ignored a tennis injury for a couple of years, and it finally found a way to catch my attention.

Fairy: Interesting that it's speaking through a back injury. I'll bet you seldom pay attention to your back.

Me: You're right. I don't pay much attention to what I can't see.

Fairy: Like me. You can't see me so you don't pay attention.

Me: If I pay attention to you, will you heal me with your elixir?

Fairy: Sure, I'll be happy to.

Me: Great! How do we get started?

Fairy: Go out in your front yard and stand with your back against that big pine tree. Ask the sap to be the elixir and to come into your lumbar 5. And don't forget to knock on wood!

Me: Thank you, Fairy. I'll try that. Do you have another word of wisdom?

Fairy: Remember that I like to come through the broken places, especially your heart. Maybe that's what you came to earth to heal.

Perhaps as a synchronicity, it wasn't long after I backed into the tree that my back began to heal. What's more, I found a helpful book, *Love in a Time of Broken Heart: Healing from Within.* Author Benig Mauger, a native of Ireland, writes about how we are "looking for love in all the wrong places," as the song goes, and offers ways to love ourselves through the inner marriage.

As we learn to relate to the true self at the level of the fourth chakra, we will also begin to find our voice at the level of the fifth chakra. Revisiting the fifth cycle provides an opportunity to notice our speech patterns and how often we use our will through words. Perhaps we use sarcasm, threats, manipulation, or drama to get our way rather than tune into the sound of the true self. To open and heal the fifth chakra, consider songs that you have enjoyed over the years. One that comes to my mind is "Coal Miner's Daughter," performed by country singer

Loretta Lynn. On a visit to the Arkansas Ozarks, I even belted out this song in a cave! Soulful songs and other kinds of music that we love can evoke the muse, our creative inspiration. (Yes, *muse* and *music* come from the same root.)

While the source of creative inspiration comes from the second chakra, with the fifth chakra, we are bringing it to a higher level. We are giving our creativity a voice, whether it is through singing, writing a book, making art, or teaching a class. A CD that captures the essence of the fifth chakra is *Peace or Drama*, by Eve Fleishman. Not only did Ms. Fleishman pen her own lyrics to the songs, but she sings poignantly from the depths of her soul. She even commissioned artists to create paintings illustrating each song (see www.EveFleishman.com).

You, too, can empower your voice by envisioning what your soul is calling you to create, but for this, you will need the wisdom of the sixth chakra. You may have already noticed that the sixth chakra is similar to the third chakra in its relationship to the mental body, with the difference being the focus on the imagination. The expression "in my mind's eye" suggests that we can use the sixth chakra to visualize and imagine.

The book *On Divination and Synchronicity: The Psychology of Meaningful Chance*, by Jungian analyst Marie-Louise Van Franz, is a good source for working with the imaginal body of the sixth chakra. I used a form of divination when consulting the books *Medicine Cards* and *Inner Child Cards*. While working with the card layouts, I was guided to the animals and fairy tales that would be the right ones for each cycle. At times, it felt as if the animals and fairy tales had actually selected me!

Following the thread of synchronicity, a good book to read when revisiting the seventh cycle is *The Tao of Psychology: Synchronicity and the Self* by Jungian analyst Jean Shinoda Bolen. The more you tune into the seventh chakra, the more you may notice synchronistic events, and then it seems as though you have been heard by the cosmos. The level of the seventh, or crown, chakra is more transcendent in nature. In fact, the power of prayer and the ability to work miracles may come from the crown chakra, which is probably why we are taught to bow our heads in reverence when we pray.

As you spiral into the cosmic realm of the eighth chakra, you may begin to receive messages about your destiny as a "lightworker." When you receive these messages, be sure to ground yourself in the first chakra. One pitfall of creative and intuitive people is going out of the body for inspiration, setting up the perfect storm for mental and physical "dis-ease." Like the lotus, we are plants that need the rich soil of earth for our soul seeds to germinate. As I was revisiting this cycle, a book caught my attention: *The Lineage of the Codes of Light* by Jesse E. Ayani. Through story, this book suggests that the matrilineal bloodline holds codes of light in the DNA and that these codes are being activated as our destiny evolves. DNA is often depicted as a rainbow spiral and may actually be the source of the rainbow body.

In the ninth cycle, the rainbow body will likely send "lightworker" messages through dreams. One night during this cycle, I had a dream so bright and vivid that it woke me up with a start: red, yellow, and green were arcing through my dream space as a voice whispered, "These are the colors you need to work with." Since red, yellow, and green are the colors of the first, third, and fourth chakras, I began to pay more attention to them. Working with the chakra colors throughout the cycles can contribute to keeping us healthy. For example, "the rainbow diet" is based on eating a food from each color group every day.

Another way to work with the colors is to visualize a particular color permeating an area of the body that needs healing. Although sources vary, here is a general guideline of the areas of the body that would benefit by visualizing a color.

- *red*: bladder, feet, legs, large intestines, male genitalia;
- *orange*: kidneys, small intestines, spleen, bones, spine, female genitalia;
- *yellow*: pancreas, liver, gallbladder, stomach;
- *green*: lungs, heart, immune system;
- *blue*: throat, jaw, tongue, teeth, lips, salivary glands, lymph glands;
- *indigo*: eyes, ears, nose, sinuses;
- *violet*: hair, scalp, brain.

I also recommend that you dialogue with the ailing area of the body so that guidance from your soul offers a healing symbol or message and brings forth meaning to the suffering.

Even though the rainbow colors are classically assigned to the seven main chakras, your soul may give you guidance for working with the colors in different ways. A book that suggests adding silver to each chakra color is *Cell-Level Healing: The Bridge from Soul to Cell* by Joyce Whiteley Hawkes. This book explores ways to use the chakra colors for regeneration on the cellular level.

Spiraling around the cycles on the Wheel of the Year is a powerful way to align your soul with the soul of the earth. As you become more connected to the soul of the natural world, you may get in touch with the grief that we all feel upon occasion though we can't quite pinpoint its origin. A pervasive and subtle undercurrent, this grief is a message that the soul of the earth is in jeopardy. When the soul is removed from the world, our institutions can become sick and toxic. A book that sheds light on this subject is *The Return of the Feminine and the World Soul* by Llewellyn Vaughn-Lee. The author states with some urgency that we must find ways to reconnect with our soul lest we destroy our humanity.

Meditating on feminine images is a good way to restore our connection with the soul. Black Madonna, for example, evokes shadow material in the deeper layers of the unconscious that could be destructive if we neglect or ignore it. Saint Brigit is an inspiring aspect of the soul that shines forth through our creativity and healing. The Virgin Mary harbors the seed of a new soul consciousness that is trying to be born in our time, and Sophia represents the evolving wisdom revealed in that new consciousness. As you spiral through the cycles, you may think of other inspiring feminine figures: Our Lady of Guadalupe from Mexico or Green Tara from Buddhism.

Working with the feminine figures in fairy tales is another powerful way to reconnect with the soul. These primal, archetypal stories get right to the heart of the soul's sickness, such as being mired down in an earlier stage of life or a rigid path that you might have outgrown. If you get too caught up in an intellectual interpretation of the fairy tales, though, you may miss out on the secret inner life of the unconscious. This is one reason I like to consult the *Inner Child Cards* when working with fairy tales: the pictures on the cards paint more than a thousand words of interpretation.

Travel is yet another way to reclaim the soul. When I went to Ireland, for example, I noted that its traditions and landscape bring together the seven main chakras. Irish dances tap the physicality of the first chakra; Irish songs, like "Danny Boy," stir the emotional body of the second chakra; Irish humor softens the grip of the power drive of the third chakra; emerald-green meadows nurture the heart energy of the fourth chakra; Irish storytelling elevates "blarney" to the eloquent speech of the fifth chakra; legends of leprechauns and fairy-folk evoke the imagination of the sixth chakra; and stone crosses in cemeteries link the starry realm of the seventh chakra to the power of the land. While traveling in Ireland, I experienced Celtic spirituality through the soul, rather than merely through the intellect.

As you plant soul seeds on your spiritual journey, the fruit will be creativity that comes from the true self. The final chapter of this book is a compilation of creative pieces that I have written over the years of spiraling the cycles on the Wheel of the Year. May they inspire you to bring forth a creative expression from your soul as you uncover and discover your true spiritual path!

CHAPTER TWELVE

SHARING SOUL BLOSSOMS

In this chapter, I share some of the writing pieces that have blossomed from sowing the seed of creativity. The first essay, "The Inner Banks," was written for our local Jung Society newsletter in Chapel Hill, North Carolina. It captures the essence of the first and second chakras.

The Inner Banks

When I first visited the Outer Banks of North Carolina, I was surprised by the soulful scenery there: long bridges over wide stretches of water leading into Nags Head; the rolling surf at Kitty Hawk with red flags warning of its wildness; large mounds of sand dunes at Jockey's Ridge surrounded by glistening pools of water; crape myrtle and magnolia trees blooming in profusion at the Elizabethan Gardens in Manteo. But perhaps it was the lighthouses dotting the landscape that had the most powerful pull: Currituck, Lookout, Okracoke, Bodie (pronounced "Body"), and especially Cape Hatteras.

Recognizing my projection on the lighthouses, I set out to receive the message that they might be sending. With Cape Hatteras as a model, I began by listing descriptive phrases: 1) red stone foundation; 2) both black and white spirals along the body; 3) winding steps leading to the top; 4) the beacon at the top; 5) the prism within the beacon; 6) windows overlooking the panoramic vista. This list of descriptive phrases helped me to visualize Cape Hatteras more fully before I moved into a Jungian exercise called "amplification."

Jung recommended amplification particularly for dream work, but you can also use it with any symbol or figure attracting your attention in the outer world. With amplification, you write the name of the central image in the middle of the page and then amplify, or add to, the image with associations. Given the natural beauty of the Outer Banks, I thought the shape of a flower would work well for this exercise.

At the center of the flower, I wrote the phrase "Cape Hatteras Lighthouse," followed by associations on the petals. On the first petal, I wrote "strong foundation." On the second petal came "dark and light spiraling energy." On the third petal came "house of light"; on the fourth petal, "body of light"; and on the fifth petal "beacon of light." As the petals rapidly unfurled with associations, so did my insights. *Aha*, I thought. The black spirals symbolize the shadow, while the white spirals point to rising consciousness. The beacon represents a guiding light on the path to psychic wholeness. The prism stands for refracting light within the psyche. So far, so good!

I left the Outer Banks early the next morning so that I could be back in time for my monthly Jungian study group. The leader of the group liked to include nonverbal exercises, such as drawing or sketching, but as a teacher and writer, I usually preferred the time set aside for discussion. On that day, however, I knew exactly what I would draw. Even as our leader gave instructions to draw a symbol of the self, I began to sketch the red stone foundation.

As the process unfolded, my drawing of Cape Hatteras began to take shape, with its black and white spirals flowing together around the body and its bright beacon lighting the way to consciousness. But as I paused and allowed myself to receive more images, I began to draw sand dunes with glistening pools of water around the base of Cape Hatteras. Almost without my awareness, came the trees I had admired in the Elizabethan Gardens. As my hand moved lower on the page, roots of the trees began to form deep into the dark soil on either side of the lighthouse, and suddenly a rush of energy moved within me, like one of those wild waves crashing onto the rolling surf.

I began to realize that my first attempt at drawing Cape Hatteras emerged from the ego-self, complete with a "cape" and a "hat" to adorn the persona! Upon adding the nature images, however, the drawing came more from the eco-self, the green part of the psyche that weaves together our inner nature with outer nature.

Jung believed that the power of God reveals itself not only in the realm of spirit, but in the fierce "animality" of nature both within us and outside us. Was I defending myself against the animality of nature? And was I so caught up in my outer experience that I almost missed the connection to my inner experience?

In our culture, we tend to "go straight for spirit," to value the light over the dark and intellect over instinct. We look up to the Father while we overlook the watery and instinctual realm of the Mother. In short, we split spirit and matter. But when we travel over the bridge to our "inner banks," the lighthouse becomes a symbol for bringing body, soul, and spirit back together again in a spiral dance with the earth.

This next essay, written for Carolina Health and Humor Association, is intended to capture the essence of the third chakra, which is mainly about dealing with ego issues. Although the birth of the ego was a necessary stage in human development, the ego has become so separated from the Great Mother that it now thinks it's the boss! Whenever you find yourself avoiding pain or other stressful situations, you may be caught in the grip of the ego. Humor helps to keep the ego in perspective.

The Whole Tooth

Maybe it stems from being a lifelong pain avoider, but truth to tell, I have a dental phobia. Whenever I have to go to the dentist, I am reminded of the man who telephoned his doctor's office to make an appointment. "I'm sorry," said the nurse, "but the doctor is out of town."

"Thank you," replied the man. "When will he be out of town again?"

So when I could no longer avoid making an appointment with my dentist, I decided to approach the situation with humor. What could I do to give it a little levity? Levitate out of the chair? Banter with the dentist while my mouth was being probed with all kinds of sharp instruments? Beg for laughing gas?

Laugh—that was it! I would put into practice humorist Alan Klein's suggestion to use the acronym LAUGH when under stress: L standing for "Let go," A for "Attitude," U for "You," G for "Go for it" (or was it "Get a grip, girl"?), and H for "Humor heals."

After being numbed by three shots of Novocain, I was all set for the ordeal. "Let go," I intoned. "Relax. Visualize a peaceful scene."

Then the dentist came in. "Sorry for the delay," she said, "but we're having trouble finding your crown. We think this is the one, but it was under another name. Someone at the lab must have mislabeled it. Don't worry—we'll just try it on for size, and if it fits, it's yours."

All right, A is for "Attitude." I have to change my attitude. Mistakes happen. So what if I'm wearing someone else's crown? Just go with the flow. "Well," said the dentist, "it seems you have a little decay on the tooth right beside the crown. May as well go ahead and fill it while you're numb. It's small—you won't feel a thing," she said as she set the drill on high squeal.

U big baby. U are the problem. It's like Alan Klein said, "U are Ur own worst enemy. The only person U can change is Urself."

"Now," said the dentist, "we're almost finished. All we have to do is wedge this clamp between your teeth to make some space."

U blankity, blank, blank! U lied! U said I wouldn't feel anything! Uh-oh, I was rapidly flunking LAUGH. It was time to get back on track.

Okay, "G." "Go for it." (Or was it "Grow up"?) "You're doing fine," I heard the dentist say. "Now bite down hard. No—harder. We've got to get that baby cemented in there. It seems to be a little loose. I surely do hope this is the right crown." Well, G!*#! Get real! I had better go on to "H" and think of some humor before I hyperventilate.

Jokes—that's it! I'll think of some old dentist jokes. Q. "What time is your dental appointment?" A. "Toothurty." Ha, ha. "Never go to a dentist whose office plants have died." Hee, hee. Nope—it wasn't working. All I wanted to do was get the H out of there.

Well, I tried, but some situations aren't funny no matter what. I have a dental phobia, and I'll never recover. My eighty-five-year-old aunt summed it up just right: "I was supposed to go in for a root canal," she said, "but fortunately I had a heart attack."

The fourth chakra is an invitation to move your awareness beyond the ego into the heart. The heart transmutes the instinctual energies of pain and fear into the spiritual energy of trust. It is the place where you can learn to speak "Spirit as a second language," that is, to discern the messages that spirit is sending. This essay conveys a message from the heart chakra.

The Carousel Horses

I had never before responded to Publisher's Clearing House Sweepstakes, but that particular year was not business as usual. I was in the throes of an internal paradigm shift, and just about anything that came across my path felt synchronistic. So when the sweepstakes entry came in the mail offering a year's subscription to carousel horse music boxes, I bit.

When the first music box arrived, I was enchanted by its beauty. Trimmed in pink and green ribbon-like swirls, it looked like a wedding cake. When I turned it over to press the button, "I Just Called to Say I Love You" filled the air. *That's curious,* I thought. *Sometimes I say "I just called to say I love you" to a friend or family member when we haven't talked for a while.*

The following month's carousel horse music box looked much like the first one, except that the swirls were painted gold and blue. Again, it reminded me of a wedding cake. As I pressed the button, I heard the strains of "Love Story." That made two love songs in a row. Was I possibly being wooed by some force from beyond?

When the next month's music box came, I was accustomed to its appearance: a four-inch-high porcelain horse sitting atop frosting-like layers of various colors. The colors on this music box were red and yellow. When I pressed the button, "Love Me Tender" came forth, an Elvis Presley hit from my youth. As I recalled Elvis's suggestive gyrations that so bothered my parents' generation, I wondered if this song could be about the instinct of lust being transmuted into the tender feeling of love.

The music box after that turned out to be "I Left My Heart in San Francisco." This one left me pondering, but when I remembered that San Francisco was named for Saint Francis of Assisi, I decided to look up something about his life. Here's what I found: Around 1220, Saint Francis set up the first three-dimensional nativity scene. He focused on an ox and a donkey and preached the duty of humankind to protect all of creation. Francis's devotion to the animal kingdom was so great that he wanted to have a special law to provide for the birds and the beasts. One story relates that on his deathbed, Saint Francis thanked his donkey for carrying him throughout his life, and his donkey wept.

Hmmm, I thought, *the animals represent the instincts, and Saint Francis centered the nativity scene on animals.* He even expressed appreciation to his donkey, and the donkey responded. Perhaps "I Left My Heart in San Francisco" was saying something about the divinity of the instincts when they are raised to the level of the heart.

At this point, I was growing more confident in my ability to decipher the message from spirit, and I eagerly awaited the next "horse of the month." When it arrived, I could hardly believe my ears: "Over the Rainbow." Was there ever a more soulful song? As I listened to the familiar tune coming from the music box, the yearning was so intense that I began to sing along. "Somewhere over the rainbow, way up high, there is a land that I heard of once in a lullaby." It was as though this song tapped a longing within me for a place that I had forgotten.

With the following month's music box, "Try to Remember," the synchronicity was striking. What was it that I was being called to remember? Was some ancient memory trying to come through? Heritage House, the company that makes the music boxes, may have provided a clue. Jung wrote that the Great Mother—the collective unconscious where the archetypes reside—is our heritage. It is "a land that I heard of once in a lullaby," a place that connects us to our soul. When we forget about this land, the heart feels lonely and alienated.

I was almost beyond surprise when the next music box came, "Brahms' Lullaby." Having a soothing quality, this tune is hummed by many a mother to her infant. It seemed to be saying that we are safe in the land of the Great Mother if we will but listen to her guidance. With the arrival of "The Music Box Dancer," the message was complete, and soul waltzed with spirit to the melody within my heart.

The fifth chakra is about blossoms flowering forth from the voice. For this meditation, choose any five-petal flower. I chose hibiscus because the shape of its petals lends a receptive quality.

Hibiscus Meditation

Imagine the hollow of your throat as a hibiscus flower with its five petals folded in toward the center. Inhale into the hibiscus, and meditate on the space around the throat area.

As you exhale, see the first petal gently unfolding from the center of the hibiscus. Say silently: "Send out your light. Let it surround and envelop me."

A second petal now unfurls from the center of the hibiscus. As the petal opens, say aloud: "The earth is full of goodness." With compassion, ask for the healing of the earth.

As a third petal rays outward, feel the harmony within and around you. See yourself as a reflection of this harmony. Know and affirm that earth and heaven are united as one.

A fourth petal now unfolds, and you hear a whisper: "Remember who you are." Hold yourself in compassion as you listen to the wisdom of your voice.

With the opening of the fifth petal, you hear the phrase: "Behold your true self." Now see all five petals of the hibiscus flower lifted up in praise and gratitude for the healing of the voice of your soul. And so it is!

The sixth chakra is about giving a voice to the wisdom of the true self. This active imagination dialogue among the spirit animals allows the instinctual parts of the self to affirm their truth. Imagine the animals sitting around an autumn campfire at dusk.

Me: Hello, Turkey, Dolphin, Possum, Grouse, Swan, Owl, Hawk, Crow, and Porcupine. It's great to see you all together! Now let's get to know one other. Would you go around the circle and say something about your particular medicine?

Turkey: My medicine is Give-Away. I am generous and humble.
Dolphin: My medicine is Manna. Manna is sacred breath.
Possum: My medicine is Diversion. I could win an Academy Award for my death act.

Grouse: My medicine is Sacred Spiral. I dance among the stumps and the stars.

Swan: My medicine is Grace. Grace is a gift—you don't have to earn it.

Owl: My medicine is Deception. I can spot fakes and phonies a mile away.

Hawk: My medicine is Message. The message is to honor all spiritual paths.

Crow: My medicine is Law. I won't say anything about my medicine—it's a secret.

Porcupine: My medicine is Innocence. You must become as a little child.

Me: Thank you all for sharing. Now I want you to give your medicine to one other animal here. Choose an animal that either needs the medicine or would know how to use it wisely. The last animal chosen will have the final word. Who would like to go first?

Turkey: That's a no-brainer—I love to give away my medicine. I give some of my humility to Crow. He seems to think he's above it all.

Crow: Actually, I am below it all. My Law is of the Underworld. I give my medicine to Grouse, who uses the sacred spiral to descend into the Underworld. Grouse will respect my Law.

Grouse: Thank you, Crow. I give my sacred spiral to Dolphin. She seems to know how to use the breath to spiral between the worlds.

Dolphin: Now let's see who can use my sacred breath. Of course! Possum! That fellow needs some breath all right, always playing dead when the going gets tough.

Possum: I don't mean to get defensive here, but sometimes diversion will get you out of a tight spot. I give my medicine to Swan—she has the grace to know when to use it. She must be from the South.

Swan: Yes, I'm from the great state of Virginia. I give my medicine to Hawk. He can spread the message that grace comes from both the dark and light sides of life.

Hawk: Okay, I'll forward this message on to Owl. She's the "seer of the soul" and knows that the dark has its own special kind of grace.

Owl: Frankly, I don't give a hoot for this game, but I bestow my ability to see in the dark to Porcupine. She needs to look out for the dark side—that child is way too innocent.

Me: Well, Porcupine, since you are the last one to receive a medicine, you have the final word. What do you say?

Porcupine: We are all interconnected and held through the power of love. Group hug?

The seventh and eighth chakras are more transcendental and cosmological in nature. These two chakras allow you to work with the heavenly bodies to co-create something in the physical world. In this meditation, the moon serves as a muse in the creation of a desired outcome.

The Moon as Muse

On the night of the dark new moon, look up into the sky and imagine the moon as a source teeming with potential life. Meditate on what seed you would like to plant in the darkness. Consider what you would like to see come to fruition over the next month or so.

Two or three nights following the dark new moon, a sliver of the crescent moon will appear in the sky. See this emerging light as the sprouting of the seed that you sowed on the night of the new moon. Look for clues of the sprouting in your everyday life.

As the moon waxes to half, know that part of what you have planted is still in the dark. Imagine that this dark side of the moon is filled with the potential of what you would like to see happen.

When the moon grows into the shape of an egg, imagine that it contains all that you have sown so far. See it as ripe and preparing to hatch.

During the full moon, ask for clarity about the seed you have planted. What steps can you take to help the seed blossom in your life? List these steps, and take action on at least one of them.

As the moon slowly begins to wane, note what has already taken place toward the blossoming of the seed. Write about or draw what you have noticed.

When the moon once again recedes into the night sky, give thanks for any positive changes that have taken place in your life. Know that the moon as muse will always be there for you as a creative partner.

Moon as Muse

The ninth chakra is about the integration and unity of all the chakras for healing and wholeness. This last piece is a dance with rainbow light for the healing of the earth and the soul.

The Goddess Creation Story

In the beginning was the goddess EVOL. She was void and formless, full of chaos. All of her ideas were in potential in a great black abyss—images of bears and turtles and bees, fish and flowers and trees—but she was just too busy to birth them. The goddess yearned to express herself, but she kept putting it off.

One night, EVOL got a wake-up call in the form of a dream. In her dream, a rooster was crowing: "Cock-a-doodle-doo, wake up! It's now or never. Go for it, girl!" This dream was so full of creative energy that it shook EVOL to her very roots. It was then that she began her rainbow dance.

On the first day, the goddess EVOL danced forth a deep red, the color of birthing blood. From her very being, she flooded the redness deep into the core of the earth, bestowing the life force on all the images in her womb.

On the second day, EVOL began to sort out the images: the moon and the sun, plants and planets, oceans and animals. The elemental creatures began to stir from their secret places within the earth, filling it with a vibrant creative orange.

On the third day, EVOL told the yellow sun that his fire was needed to bring forth the light of consciousness. "Okay, Sun," she said, "let's see what your fire can do." Feeling his power, the sun brought forth computers and cell phones, trucks and tall buildings, highways and byways—and human beings with their own free will.

On the fourth day, EVOL began to see trouble brewing, so she reversed the letters in her name. The goddess EVOLved into the goddess LOVE and opened up the human heart. She told the sun of her love for all creation and asked him to be her partner in this green fertile dance.

On the fifth day, the goddess and the sun sat down together to have a dialogue about the balance of power. At first, the sun wanted to keep all his power for himself, but when the goddess released the power of LOVE, a deep, healing blue entered the space between them.

On the sixth day, the goddess and the sun held a brainstorming session to come up with a vision. They would birth a new being, an expression of harmony and balance. And so it was! With her wise indigo eyes, the goddess looked upon her new creation and saw that it was very good.

On the seventh day, the goddess spun violet strands from the crown of her head to connect the stars in the Milky Way with every corner of the earth and down to its central core. As a web of white light surrounded the earth and all of the cosmos, the goddess knew that her rainbow dance was done. And then she rested.

REFERENCES

Ayani, Jesse E. *Awakening and Healing the Rainbow Body*. Mount Shasta, CA: Heart of the Sun Publishing, 2004.

Barnstone, Willis, and Marvin Meyer, eds. *The Gnostic Bible*. Boston: Shambhala Press, 2003.

Bien, Julianne. *Color: Awakening the Child Within*. Toronto: Spectrahue Light & Sound, 2007.

Bly, Robert, and Marion Woodman. *The Maiden King: The Reunion of Masculine and Feminine*. New York: Henry Holt and Company, 1998.

Chevalier, Jean, and Alain Gheerbrant. *Dictionary of Symbols*. Translated in 1994 by John Buchanon-Brown. New York: Penguin Books.

Dale, Cyndi. *The Subtle Body: An Encyclopedia of Your Energetic Anatomy*. Boulder: Sounds True, 2009.

Ferguson, Diana. *The Magickal Year: A Pagan Perspective on the Natural World*. New York: Quality Paperback Book Club, 1996.

Keim, Timothy. "Moving toward Extinction." *The Chapel Hill Herald*. May 9, 2009.

Lerner, Isha, and Mark Lerner. *Inner Child Cards: A Journey into Fairy Tales, Myth, and Nature*. Santa Fe, NM: Bear & Company Publishing, 1992.

Linn, Denise. *Altars: Bringing Sacred Shrines into Your Everyday Life*. New York: The Ballantine Publishing Group, 1999.

Marcus, Clare Cooper. *House as a Mirror of Self: Exploring the Deeper Meaning of Home*. Berkley, CA: Conari Press, 1995.

Sams, Jamie, and David Carson. *Medicine Cards*. New York: St. Martin's Press, 1988, 1999.

Seifert, Theodor. *Snow White: Life Almost Lost*. Wilmette, IL: Chiron Publications, 1986.

Tachi-ren, Tashira. *What Is Lightbody?* Lithia Springs, GA: New Leaf Distributing, 1999.

Wikman, Monika. *Pregnant Darkness: Alchemy and the Rebirth of Consciousness*. Berwick, ME: Nicolas-Hays, Inc., 2004.

Woodman, Marion, and Elinor Dickson. *Dancing in the Flames: The Dark Goddess in the Transformation of Consciousness*. Boston: Shambhala Publications, 1997.